CW00498663

Feng Shui

This is a Parragon Book
This edition published in 2003

Parragon
Queen Street House
4 Queen Street
Bath BA1 1HE, UK

ISBN: 1-40540-274-1

A copy of the CIP data for this book is available from the British
Library upon request.

Editorial, design and layout by Essential Books

Printed and bound in China

Feng Shui

Jo Russell

CONTENTS

Introduction

What is Feng Shui?

Feng Shui is the term given to the harnessing of natural energy (Chi or Qi) that emanates from the heavens and earth. If we live and spend time in an area that generates positive vibrations, own levels of personal energy increase. In time, our reserves of energy are compounded by the natural resources, the Chi, promoting good fortune and favourable opportunities. In turn we are able to think, see and act more clearly, with confidence and conviction.

There are many components to consider when you begin to alter the Feng Shui of your home or office. This book has been designed to simplify some of the ancient formulas that hold the secrets to great good fortune, including wealth and prosperity, health for yourself, contentment for your family and personal happiness.

How Does It Work?

There is often confusion about Chi, or energy, probably due to the fact that it is invisible, with no apparent source or final destination and is linked to many mystical and magical theories including the everlasting question, the meaning of life. Energy has long been recognised as a powerful entity, without substance or form; we are aware of something, yet we find it difficult to accept why it exists and how it really works. Science has been trying to prove and understand the dynamics of energy, with new technology being used to monitor split atoms and decode DNA, yet still there has been no conclusive proof of what energy actually is and where it comes from. Many religions and philosophies accept the idea of a powerful force that come from the heavens and the earth. Feng Shui is a natural approach, which readily accepts natural energy lines, understanding how they operate.

Over thousands of years, the ancient Chinese observed the stars and the relationship they have with the seasons and the earth. Roughly 5000 years ago formulas were evolved which provide the roots to Feng Shui. These formulas enable a person to live in tune with natural energy lines, known as 'The Veins of the Dragon'. Once a person has finely tuned their home to the positive natural vibrations (Sheng Chi) and is able to live in harmony with the Chi that accompanies their surroundings, they become empowered. This boost to their own personal energy will increase extremely favourable opportunities, good health, harmonic relationships, wealth and prosperity. Likewise, if they are living in an area which is breeding negative vibrations (Shar Chi) their own energy resources will become infected. Left unattended this type of energy will exhaust a person, they will begin to feel tired and drained. Slowly this will spread until they become unwell, unable to cope, and begin to have difficulties with relationships, financial worries and stress-related problems. In the most extreme of cases, Shar Chi is the energy associated with death.

Principally, Feng Shui techniques are applied to harmonise homes, offices and gardens, to encourage opportunities and good fortune. It is the attunement with invisible fields of energy that will bring auspicious Chi to those who are in contact with such an environment.

Another way of understanding Feng Shui is that it increases your awareness of your environment and helps you recognise the parallel it represents to your life. If your home is neglected, it is highly likely that the same neglect has over-spilled into other areas of your life. By spending periods of time in positive surroundings, you will experience a growing feeling of wellbeing and make the most of the opportunities that come your way.

Modern Application of Feng Shui

The culture of ancient China is still very much intact today. For centuries, the secrets of many fascinating subjects including Chinese traditional medicine, Tai Chi, Feng Shui, astrology and divination have been passed on to each successive generation with a high regard for their importance and the effects they have on daily life.

As we rocket into the twenty-first century, there is an increasing emphasis on technology and materialism. Yet in the western world there appears to be a growing unease regarding the happiness and wellbeing of our future and the future of our children. Balance is crucial to our survival, by applying the wisdom of ancient China to the glory of modern technology, we are able to bring together the two dual forces of nature, yin and yang, and thereby become whole once more.

Balance and harmony are the key components to successful Feng Shui. The objective is to make your home, office or garden as pleasing as possible.

Chi is the universal force of energy that penetrates everything. Chi is continually moving, swirling in and around objects. The most auspicious Chi, Sheng Chi, moves gently in curves, it is this Chi that is the easiest to harness and one that turns into favourable opportunities. For Feng Shui purposes it is this Chi that is encouraged in the home, office and garden.

Chi will follow the shape or direction of an object and it gathers speed and momentum if the object is long, straight or sharp. Should an object be spiky or covered in jagged edges the Chi becomes fragmented and splintered. This type of energy, Shar Chi, is dangerous and will affect the personal energy of everyone who comes into contact with it. Over a long period of time, this energy will cause harm to the health and fortune of those in its presence. Feng Shui works to avoid or negate this kind of negative energy.

Where It All Begins

The Three Trinities of Luck

Feng Shui is not a spell that will magically transform your life. To make Feng Shui work for you it is important to realise that it works in conjunction with two other subtle energy types. This combination is based on the Chinese Philosophy of the Three Trinities of Luck, which are:

> **Tien Chai** – Heaven Luck – Astrology
> **Ti Chai** – Earth Luck – Feng Shui
> **Ren Chai** – Man Luck – The Person You Are

Tien Chai – Heaven Luck

This is known as your fate or destiny and is a form of astrology. Known as the Four Pillars of Destiny, it takes into account the available elemental energies at the exact moment that you were born. This will make every person's Heavens Luck individual and unique to them

The Three Trinities of Luck

and through it you can view a map of your life. This can be applied to advanced levels of Feng Shui Schools to personalise a Feng Shui environment.

On average, each person will have an equal measure of good and bad luck; this luck will normally rise and fall, giving peaks and troughs to our lives. We all experience days when just about everything seems to go wrong, while on other days we wake up and it is as if the sun is shining on us personally and everything seems to flow perfectly. Our fate and destiny is beyond our control, there are some things which are just meant to be. We are all unique in our own way and that is what makes life so interesting. Life would be very dull if there wasn't any way to gauge the depth of our achievements by the level of our successes and failures.

We cannot change our Heaven Luck as we cannot alter the date and time that we were born but if we have our astrology read we can be prepared and can maximise the changes to our destiny.

Ti Chai – Earth Luck

The second part of the trilogy is known as your Earth Luck or, in other words, the Feng Shui of your environment. If the energy levels around your home are in harmony and balanced, it is possible to say that your home has positive Feng Shui. Earth energy will take into account the surrounding landscape, the health of the surrounding plants and abundance of natural light and wildlife, and the directions of nearby waterways.

The most important aspect of the Earth Luck, or the Feng Shui of your environment, is that we are able to manipulate it to our own advantage by implementing changes. If an area is dark, damp and gloomy, we can take positive steps to improve the space by creating more light, opening airflows, changing the colours and adding fresh flowers to transform the Chi and create positive energy. Therefore with a little effort and plenty of know-how we can create wonderful living conditions which will have a growing effect on our health, moods and natural energy levels. We are responsible for our environment. Instead of challenging nature we should recognise, respect and respond to it as much as possible.

It is impossible to reach one hundred per cent perfect Feng Shui as there is always an amount of yin and yang inside everything. However it is possible to maximise the energy through our own making. Therefore we could easily increase the positive flow of energy in our homes and businesses by up to ninety per cent.

Ren Chai – Man Luck

The third and final part of the trilogy is Man Luck. As man is found between the heavens and the earth, he or she is responsible for actions of his or her own making, this is known as having Man Luck or free will.

The way that you perceive yourself, others and the decisions that you are faced with daily are part of the trilogy of forces that control your destiny. You are responsible for creating a third of your own luck. We are faced with questions, choices and decisions every second of the day, absorbing, analysing and processing information. Our temper will reflect our moods, in turn altering our behaviour. Therefore if we are feeling happy and positive we are more likely to be successful. We are living in a tough and competitive society with pressures building and competition high, and increasingly we are forced to make snap decisions.

The quality of our life and our relationships with others is based on our wellbeing. If we are unhappy or unsatisfied in our expectations, we are more likely to resort to dealing with these aspects in anger, jealousy or blame. People around us, whether they are friends, family or colleagues, will eventually resent or even dislike the way that we behave. Their reaction to us will fuel an ever-widening cycle of bitterness and misunderstanding. The more unfulfilled and unhappy we become, the greater the chances of responding from a negative viewpoint. Therefore it is essential that we are able to reach and understand a higher perspective of happiness and wellbeing. If we understand that our moods come not just from external factors but also from ourselves, the way we see ourselves and others, it is easier to change our viewpoint and take responsibility for our actions.

The more you draw from your personal wisdom, the greater the benefit you will reap. It is the application of your education and your experiences that creates wisdom. What is the use of a lesson from a book if you do not put it into daily practice? It remains locked away, hidden and unused, left to become dusty and forgotten. The same can be said of a person who continually makes the same mistakes over and over again, they fail to see that they are in a pattern of misery, they have not learnt from their experiences and instead deflect the responsibilities of their actions by blaming others.

It is important to understand that Feng Shui cannot possible work by itself without support from you and the surrounding landscape. It is your awareness and consciousness which works hand in hand with the magic of Feng Shui. There are secrets that work in invisible ways that cannot be explained, they simply work, but it is a joint exercise between the environment and the person living in it that makes the combination effective. It will not provide instant results, like winning the lottery overnight, but works on a much deeper and subtler level. If you raise your awareness and increase the quality of the Chi around you, opportunities stand out brightly and you can present yourself as a confident and strong person, able to reach your full potential and maximise the results of these opportunities.

Feng Shui needn't be hard work, but the results that you obtain are linked to the amount of effort and time you are willing to make. The work should not be done just for personal gain either, it is important to realise that Feng Shui is related to harmony and balance. To make the utmost of the benefits that Feng Shui will bring, you must extend the energy positively to others, increasing the feel-good factor.

With the benefit of Feng Shui added to our growing awareness, determination and positive attitude we are able to achieve absolutely anything that we set our hearts on. If we do not activate our Man Luck most of the Feng Shui energy will pass through our fingers like little fishes in a stream, onwards to the next person who is perhaps more ready, willing and able.

Yin and Yang

Understanding Yin and Yang

The Chinese philosophy regarding the meaning behind life begins with the concept that everything in the universe, heaven and earth, is composed of two cosmic forces. These forces are equal and yet exactly opposite to each other. They are known as yin and yang. Together they form the 'Tao' or 'Way', when everything is balanced and in harmony. They are illustrated by the symbol 'Tai Chi'.

The sphere is formed from two colours, black and white, entwined together with a small dot of the other colour found in each side. This simple symbol represents the meaning of life, showing that there are two dual forces of nature, forever changing, one never fully obscuring the other and representing the opposites of everything. You cannot have one side without the other. It is impossible to have one hundred per cent yin or one hundred per cent yang, for even when one energy type is at its most powerful or extreme, there will always be a tiny amount of the other, as represented by the two dots found inside the symbol.

Yin and yang symbolises opposites; not only in the physical world but also in emotions, activities, sounds, and behaviour. Absolutely everything can be measured in terms of yin and yang.

Understanding Yin and Yang

Yin	Yang
Dark, Moon, Night, Feminine, Passive, Soft, Cold, Winter, Wet, Quiet, Gentle, Earth, Mother, Death, Black, Sorrow	Light, Sun, Day, Masculine, Active, Hard, Hot, Summer, Dry, Loud, Abrasive, Heaven, Father, Life, Red, Joy

When implementing Feng Shui it is crucial to have an understanding of how the yin and yang concept can be applied to your surroundings. Your objective is to create a positive environment; you want to create a balance between yin and yang, which in turn leads to harmony, encouraging good fortune.

With a pen and paper, walk around the area to be consulted and jot down whatever comes to mind, this will give you an idea of what degree of yin energy and yang energy is available in your home, office and garden. For example, if the area were very dark with little or no natural light in it, it would be considered very yin. If the area were very bright with plenty of windows and little or

no shade, the energy would be more yang. If there is an extreme of either yin or yang, then there will be an imbalance, which will manifest itself in negative energy. Left unattended, this negative energy will have far-reaching effects, causing behavioural problems, insecurity, missed opportunities, illness and even loss of finances.

Yin and yang levels vary through the seasons, the yang energy is most powerful in the summer, in the winter yin energy is dominant, and the spring and autumn are the transition seasons.

Spring slowly gathers more yang energy until it becomes summer and the yin aspect is at its weakest level. Autumn is the season in which the yang energy starts to ebb away, giving in to yin energy. This can be seen physically, as the days become longer and warmer during the summer and shorter and darker during the winter.

Another example of where yin and yang can be seen clearly is in restaurants:

Macdonald's restaurants are very active with shiny reflective surfaces. The colours are bright red and yellow and the levels of lighting are high. The emphasis is on fast food with the customer encouraged to buy, eat and then leave the restaurant as quickly as possible in order to make room for the next customer. This type of restaurant is extremely yang. The food is inexpensive as profits are met by a high turnover.

By contrast a quiet, subdued restaurant with dimmed lights and soft music is creating a receptive and passive atmosphere designed to encourage the customers to relax and stay for longer and to spend more money. This type of restaurant makes a positive use of yin energy. Though there will be fewer customers, the prices will be more expensive than those in fast food chains.

Both systems are designed to make money for the restaurant owners but they have two opposite approaches. One has an emphasis on yang energy the other is using yin.

As energy is constantly moving and changing from yin to yang following the cycles of time, it will be necessary to take the time dimension into consideration. Eventually some of the Feng Shui of your home or

Understanding Yin and Yang

business will need to be adapted over long periods. For example, a small tree will eventually grow into a large tree, this will have an effect on your fortune if you used the tree as a Feng Shui enhancer.

The Five Elemental Forces of Nature

Energy can also be described in terms of the five elements or elemental effects of natural phenomenon. Nature is comprised of five subtle types of energy as well as yin and yang. As everything in the universe is composed of yin and yang, so too will everything be influenced by the five elements.

The five elements are Fire, Earth, Metal, Water and Wood. These elements can be used to describe seasons, colours, numbers, parts of the body, taste, astrology, shape, in fact everything can be viewed in elemental terms. For Feng Shui purposes the objective is to obtain harmony and balance between the five elements.

The theory behind the five elements is used in all schools of Feng Shui as well as traditional Chinese Medicine and an understanding of the difference between them and of what they represent is crucial for a Feng Shui consultation.

Fire

This element is associated with summer, the colour red, the number nine and the south. It is extremely yang in nature and is connected to warmth, romance, joy and laughter. It also represents spontaneity, recognition and fame. The yang aspect would be similar to the energy created by the fire in a furnace; the yin aspect can be compared to the flame from a candle. Yang fire would be red or purple whereas yin fire would be pink.

The Five Elemental Forces of Nature

In the body, the brain, heart, blood and nervous system are all governed by the fire element.

Earth

This is a grounding element, in the seasons it is the element that acts as a transition between summer through to autumn and winter to spring. The colours yellow, beige and shades of brown are associated with this element as are the numbers two, five and eight. The directions that are linked to the earth element are southwest and northeast, together with the centre of a building. You would use this element for increasing stability, strength and support. Another use would be for increasing the energy for comfort and security. The yang aspect would be the energy associated with the majesty of a mountain whereas the yin aspect is compared to that of the soil, stones, crystals and ceramics.

In the body, the stomach, digestive organs, cells and body fat are represented by the earth element.

Metal

The metal element represents with the season of autumn. Metallic objects and colours and the colour white are associated with this element. The metal element provides structure and organisation to an area. Its energy is calm and collected, clear and precise. The numbers six and

The Five Elemental Forces of Nature

seven are associated with this element as are the compass directions west and northwest.

Another aspect of this element is its power in networking and connecting. Imagine all the wires used in communication, this industry would have a powerful influence from the metal element. The yang aspect of this element would be comparable to a steel girder providing structure and support to a building or the energy associated with weapons. The yin aspect is more delicate and associated with wires or jewellery.

In the body, the lungs, skin and teeth are governed by the metal element.

Water

This element is the most yin out of all of the five elements, as a season it is associated with winter and the colours black and blue. The number one and the compass direction of north represent it. The water element is used to describe objects that are wet, damp and cold. It is associated with all aspects of liquids and fluids. Natural phenomenon such as streams, rain, waterfalls and oceans are all represented by this element, as are manmade objects such as swimming pools and bathrooms.

In behaviour, water is used to describe a person who is deep, perhaps an intellectual. Water is a popular Feng Shui enhancer as it is the presence of water that represents purity and the source of life, since without water life could not exist. The yang aspect of this element is associated with a large expanses of water such as the ocean, whereas the yin aspect is compared to the dew on a blade of grass.

In the body, the kidneys, bones and reproductive organs are represented by the water element.

The Five Elemental Forces of Nature

The Five Elemental Forces of Nature

Wood

The season that is associated with the wood element is spring. It represents new growth and new beginnings. Green is the colour that represents this element, as are the numbers three and four. The compass directions for the wood element are east and southeast. This is a caring and gentle element, it is also associated with growing wealth and prosperity and therefore is a very popular as a Feng Shui enhancer. The yang aspect of this element would be that of an established mature tree or a heavy piece of wooden furniture. The energy associated with the yin aspect is that of a flower. Stubborn behaviour is linked with yang wood whereas yin wood is flexible.

In the body, the arms and legs, liver and spinal cord are governed by the wood element.

The five elements can be used to create balance in conjunction with the yin and yang theory. This will give depth to the energy in your home to make the Feng Shui even more effective. For example, if you have a room that is very dark, it would be considered too yin. For Feng Shui purposes you would need to increase the yang aspect. You could add a light, but if you were also to add a red accessory such as a rug or a picture, you would be adding the fire element to the same area. Fire is associated with warmth and the summer, so, again, you would be increasing the yang energy. The energy of the room would begin to feel more balanced and in harmony and you would have improved the Feng Shui of that area.

Another example would be an extremely bright room with plenty of windows where yang energy was dominant. To increase the balance without blocking off the light you could add cooler tones such as blue or black accessories that increase the yin levels of the Chi and in turn provide harmony. This room would then become balanced, thereby becoming a comfortable and relaxing area to spend time in and you would not lose any light.

To apply the relationships between the elements, first become familiar with the colours that they represent. This will then act as a simple and inexpensive tool for

The Five Elemental Forces of Nature

changing the energy in your home or offices without the need for structural improvements.

The Elements and Their Colours

Earth	Metal	Water	Wood	Fire
Yellow	White	Black	Green	Red
Brown	Gold, Silver	Navy		Pink
Beige	Metallic colours			Purple

The Constructive and Destructive Cycles

The five elements can be arranged into two different cycles, which show how the elements interact with one another. The cycles are known as the Constructive Cycle and the Destructive Cycle.

The elements are able to control one another by either being able to produce an element, as seen in the Constructive Cycle, or being able to destroy another element, as in the Destructive Cycle.

The Constructive Cycle of elements is used to give strength and support to any of the elemental forces that are weak or missing from the Feng Shui of your space.

The Destructive Cycle of elements works in a similar way to the Constructive Cycle, however instead of giving birth or support to another element, this cycle shows how each element is capable of weakening and eventually destroying another element. It can be used to

The Constructive and Destructive Cycles

reduce dominant forces from the Feng Shui of your space.

Each element is only able to give birth to one particular element and, equally, only able to destroy one particular element.

The Constructive Cycle

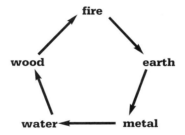

Beginning with the top of the cycle: whenever the fire element becomes extreme it will create the earth element. This can be seen in nature, as a fire will produce ash.

Earth in turn is capable of producing the metal

element. Under pressure the earth will condense minerals into metal ore, which is mined from the ground.

Metal is the element that gives birth to the water element. This transition is more obscure than the others, however, when you place metal under extreme conditions, such as high heat (yang) the metal will turn into a liquid. Likewise when you place metal into freezing (yin) conditions, the molecules that make up metal will retract and attract miniature drops of condensation.

Water is the element that feeds and nourishes the wood element, as can be seen daily in nature, where plants will wilt and eventually die if they are starved of water.

Wood is the element that gives birth to the fire element, just as logs are used to fuel a fire.

The Constructive and Destructive Cycles

The Destructive Cycle

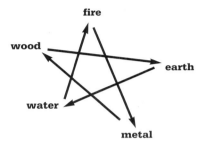

Starting with the fire element it is possible to see that this element is capable of reducing and eventually destroying the power of the metal element. As more heat is applied to metal, its structure and strength is reduced until finally it becomes a pool of liquid. An understanding of this energy can be useful as the application of heat in a controlled environment will enable the metal element to become flexible enough to be moulded and shaped into a useful object, such as shoes for a horse or wires for communication.

The metal element has the power to control and eventually destroy the wood element as an axe can cut into and eventually fell a tree. In terms of usefulness it is a controlled application of the metal element that gives society carved wooden furniture and, on a smaller scale, allows us to shape an untidy plant in the garden.

The wood element has the power to absorb and finally destroy the earth element. Imagine the power of tree roots as they worm their way though the soil, searching for water and nutrients. Eventually, without any mulch to replenish the soil, the earth is exhausted by the energy of the wood element and left barren.

Earth is the element that has the power to control and destroy the water element. It will absorb water. Imagine a glass of clear fresh water, this water would become undrinkable when mixed with sand or soil.

The water element is the element that has the power to control and then finally distinguish the fire element. When used in moderation this application has positive results, for example in the production of steam, which, when harnessed properly, can be used to power a steam

The Constructive and Destructive Cycles

engine. On a smaller scale, water, when heated, is beneficial for cooking. However, to use these energies together takes careful monitoring and should never be taken for granted.

The Destructive Cycle is useful if you have an overwhelming influence of a particular element. For example, a white office, filled with electrical equipment, will provide an overwhelming level of the metal element. A person spending a long period of time in this energy field will soon feel tension in the neck and shoulders and will quickly become drained. To relieve the pressure of the metal element, use the Destructive Cycle to create an outlet. Plants in red pots, or a shade of green on the walls will provide a calming influence as they introduce the wood and fire elements into the area.

Interpreting the five elements in your home or office will take some practice. The initial step is to recognise objects in their elemental terms. To make this exercise easier, walk around your home with a pen and paper and make a lists of everything, especially large pieces of furniture,

under headings for each element. For example, your list
might look something like this.

Fire	Earth	Metal
Red rug	Yellow hall	White room
Oven	Crockery	Computer
Fireplace	Ceramic vase	Wind chime
Water	**Wood**	
Blue furnishings	Green furnishings	
Aquarium	Bunch of flowers	
Picture of	Wood cabinet	
water scene		

Remember, the key to Feng Shui is balance and harmony,
if your home is lacking in one element, it will create a
disturbance. This could be the cause of low levels of
personal energy, personal problems or ill health.

The Constructive and Destructive Cycles

Elements and Time

In the relation to time, Chi is always moving and the strength of each element will change with the cycle of time.

Seasons are allocated elements, as are hours, days, and months and years, in fact time can be measured by using the five elements, as they constantly revolve in their endless cycles.

In the calendar, February and March are known as wood element months. April is a transition month between spring and summer and is associated with the earth element. May and June are related to the fire element. July is another earth element as the season turns to autumn. August and September are metal months, with October as another earth month. At the end of October the winter season starts with November and December being the water element months. January is an earth element month as it represents the transition from winter to spring.

The Chinese begin the New Year in the beginning of February, which is the birth of spring.

Just as every month and season is allocated an element, so too are years measured in elemental terms. For example, the year 2000 is the year of the Yang Metal Dragon. A person born during this year would be very sensitive to the metal element, especially if they were born in either August or September. It would be advisable to gently increase the water, fire and wood elements in their surroundings to give the metal energy an outlet. The outcome will be element balance, which will lead to good health, caring relationships and increased opportunities for wealth and happiness.

Other examples of using time dimension with the five elements and Feng Shui are:

- A person born in a fire year will be sensitive to the metal, water and earth elements. If they are experiencing bad luck and feeling weak, look at their home, and find out which elements are in abundance and which elements are weak or missing. To give support, increase the colours red, pink, purple (for fire) and the colour green (for wood) in their décor. It would also be effective to increase the levels of light,

The Constructive and Destructive Cycles

either natural or through other forms of lighting, as this is also associated with the fire element. To add plants to the space will increase the wood element as will choosing wood as a material to use for furniture – wood is the element which gives birth to fire. If, on the other hand, the fire energy is too strong, it will be necessary to provide an outlet with the metal, water and earth elements to reduce the intensity of the fire element.

- A person born in an earth year will need support from the earth and fire elements, so add shades of yellow through to brown and shades of red to their surroundings. When the earth is too strong, and therefore extreme, it will become negative, therefore increase the wood, metal and water elements as these elements will reduce the earth and act as an outlet, thereby creating a balance.

For a full accurate diagnosis of the elements that were available at the exact moment that you were born, it is necessary to have a Chinese Horoscope, known as the Four Pillars of Destiny.

To give an element strength and durability it is important to give it support from the Constructive Cycle. Likewise, if an element is overly dominant, then it is important to give it an outlet before there is a negative reaction, so increase an element from the Destructive Cycle.

Follow the two Cycles of the Elements to determine which elements you will need for element Chi balancing. Experiment with different colours in your clothing, to find which suit you and make you feel stronger and which leave you feeling drained, then you can apply this information to your home.

The Feng Shui Schools

There are several schools of Feng Shui, and this can lead the beginner into chaos and confusion. It is possible to use more that one school, as they can work in conjunction with one another. The two most popular and simple schools are the Form and Landscape School and the Compass School. They work together and have proved to be successful and simple schools that require little if any maintenance once the formulas have been activated.

This section of the book will bring an insight into the more popular schools used by Feng Shui practitioners. Do not expect instant results when you apply the methods described, but do keep up your awareness by recognising the increase in your good fortune, and grasp the new opportunities with a tight grip when they come towards you.

The first confusion of newcomers to Feng Shui often arises when they are confronted by Yin House Feng Shui or Yang House Feng Shui. Both schools are popular in the Far East, where there is a great emphasis on protecting and honouring the spirits of departed ancestors.

Yin House Feng Shui is a very specialised school and is mainly practised in the Far East by a few Feng Shui masters. Yin energy is associated with stillness, quiet, death and spirituality and Yin House Feng Shui is used to provide a protected and auspicious burial site for the spirit of the departed ancestors. This act will bring the favoured fortune of the departed spirit to the living members of his or her family. As the energy will affect the descendants of the family, and because there is so much respect for the elder members of the family, a great emphasis is put on providing the best possible grave site.

Yang House Feng Shui follows a different system to that of Yin House Feng Shui. Yang energy represents activity, life, movement and growth and it is Yang House Feng Shui that is used to provide auspicious energy for the living, in their surroundings, homes and businesses. It is this school that is discussed in further detail in this book.

The Feng Shui Schools

There are several branches to Yang House Feng Shui, such as the Form and Landscape School and the Compass School, which affect the landscape around the property, the building itself, the interior and finally the people living in the building. Understanding the different schools may sound like a huge amount of work, but as you will see, the formulas are simple and effective, and are quick to implement.

Preparation – Removing Clutter and Space Clearing

Though a powerful and liberating exercise, the removal of clutter should not be confused with, or replace, the rules of Feng Shui. However, to remove unwanted articles from your home, wardrobe and life will improve your Feng Shui as it makes room for new ideas and developments. It will also reduce the risk of negative Chi gathering in the dust and piles of 'To do later' jobs, and should therefore always be encouraged. As Chi is influenced by everything it encounters as it moves in and around your house, it makes practical sense to keep your home tidy and free of annoying or useless articles. This will ensure that the Chi that you are tapping into will be as positive as possible. Removal of clutter will improve the results of the Feng Shui cures or enhancers that you choose to use in your home.

'Space clearing' is another exercise that works on cleaning the energy of your home or business. Space clearing is useful if you have moved into a new home and the atmosphere feels heavy or dull, or if the air in the room feels stale. It is also helpful to 'clear' the space of a room or house after there has been an argument or trauma, as this type of negative energy will leave invisible imprints in the building. Subconsciously, we are able to receive these vibrations and will be influenced by them. If a building has been witness to a tragedy or trauma, the energy of that event will be absorbed into the walls by the receptive earth element (all buildings and property are associated with the earth element). Therefore cleansing a building will release stuck or stagnant energy. There are several techniques that are used to replace stale and stagnant energy with fresh and positive energy.

Some Simple Space Clearing Techniques

- Open two windows in the room to be cleared. This will create an air flow and will allow fresh Chi to enter the building.

- Remove all trace of dust, cobwebs and debris from corners and dark spaces.
- Use either a candle or lamp to increase the light in these areas.
- Waft incense or aromatherapy oils in corners and rooms that have experienced unhappy or stagnant energy.
- Use sound. This could be pure sound such as a bell or singing bowl; it could also be a favourite piece of music or a rhythm made from clapping.
- Use movement. Dance, wave your arms and chant, any movement that you make will remove stale Chi.
- Do any or all of the exercises when you are feeling happy, grounded and focused, you do not want to remove one level of anxiety to replace it with another.

Removing clutter and space clearing are simple yet powerful antidotes for reducing tension and negative Chi; they should be used in conjunction with Feng Shui, but do not expect results by space clearing alone.

Exterior Feng Shui – Form and Landscape School

Form School is perhaps the most important school of Feng Shui as it interprets the physical aspects of the landscape and buildings of your environment. The land forms, shapes, waterways and neighbouring hills, mountains and buildings generate energy from the earth that affects the Feng Shui of your environment. The quality of the auspicious energy generating in and around your building will have an effect on the cures or enhancers that you place in the interior of your home or office.

With a negative landscape, the Feng Shui that you apply inside your property will work at a much slower rate and the effect will be minimised. Therefore to make Feng Shui as powerful and as effective as possible, always pay close attention to the landscape around the building that is to be consulted, including other buildings, roads, junctions, hills, mountains, walls and hedges. To make sure that there is nothing left out, walk around with your pen and paper making a note of all outstanding features. This will give you invaluable information for your analysis.

Awareness of Our Surroundings

Feng Shui is an ancient art, perhaps over 5,000 years old, the secrets and messages that were important to civilisation then are just as important now.

It has been possible to translate and interpret the codes, poetry and symbols of ancient manuscripts and texts into solid and effective analysis and formulas, the results of which have been proven successful by people all over the world.

The main differences that we have to take into account from the ancient to the modern world are the manmade changes to our environment. Buildings and roads have substituted mountains and rivers, but the movement of Chi remains the same. Today, consideration must be given to many modern structures such as telegraph poles, high rise-buildings, flyovers and T-junctions.

Modern technology sees us, literally, flying into the future; our working and home lives are affected by computer technology, digital communication and e-commerce. To avoid our lives becoming sterile as we hurtle our way through our future, it is essential that we don't lose our roots with nature. Practising Feng Shui is a way to connect with this natural energy and ensure that our lives are balanced.

The shape of the world is continually shifting and changing, so too must our awareness of the implications that it has on our health and wellbeing. As our wisdom grows with tools such as Feng Shui, we are able not only to cope but also to take positive steps to improving our future.

Yin and Yang in the Landscape

The principles of yin and yang are your first indication of what type of energy is around you. The crucial factor for creating harmony using earth's energy is balance. This rule also applies to location. Ideally the home will be situated in an area that is neither too yang or too yin. For example, an area that is flat without any visible form of life would be considered extremely yin. If the area consisted of a high mountainous range with a fast-flowing waterfall rushing close by to your home, it would be considered extremely yang. Both would be equally inhospitable.

On a more subtle level, the yin and yang rules can be applied to the level of activity or stillness in the location. The perfect location will have an equal balance between both types of energy, this will mean living in a quiet, clean residential area, away from noisy traffic or busy buildings, such as a school, shopping centre or factories.

Combating Excessive Ying Energy in the Landscape

If your home is situated near a graveyard, it would be deemed as being inauspicious, as a grave site is an area which will generate an overwhelming amount of yin energy due to its association with death. This is also true of areas in the close vicinity of churches and hospitals, which carry yin energy relating to sickness and death.

There are steps that you can take for rebalancing. It will be imperative for you to make the part of your home that overlooks the unfavourable area as yang and as attractive as possible. Under no circumstances allow this area to become neglected, dirty, dark or damp, as you will be accumulating high levels of yin energy which will over-spill into and infect the lives and fortune of the inhabitants of the building.

To raise yang energy, paint the front door bright red and keep outside lights on twenty-four hours a day. Another cure would be to hide or block the offending area from view with a wall or hedge. However, do keep walls and hedges in proportion to your property, otherwise you will achieve an effect similar to that of imprisonment.

Combating Excessive Yang energy in the Landscape

If you are living above a busy street in an active part of town, you may suffer the effects of excessive yang energy, such as noise pollution from the constant roar of traffic. To counteract the negative implications it will be necessary to increase the yin energy of your home.

Use dark colours such as black or navy in the areas where the yang energy is accumulating. Hanging long, heavy and dark curtains at the windows will absorb extreme yang energy at the point where it enters the room. Indeed, for practical reasons, it would be wise to use heavy curtains that will act as a buffer between the street and the interior of the room.

Soft, rounded furniture in cool tones and colours will create an atmosphere of peace and quiet. Pictures of water or an internal water fountain will reduce stress and calm nerves.

Keep the lighting levels low and atmospheric; use table lamps to lift dark corners.

Form School Shapes Using the Five Elements

Another important element to interpreting your environment is the shape of the land formations, waterways and buildings. The shape of any formation can be described in elemental terms:

Earth

This will be a solid shape, normally square. When describing a hill or building, an earth object will be fairly square in shape, such as a hill with a plateau. When considering the bends and direction of a stream or river, the earth element is given to those bends that are square or ones that have bends that are roughly at ninety degrees.

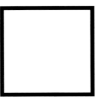

Metal

This will be circular. Areas which include domes, either in the ceiling or in doorways, are given metal energy attributes. A metal hill or building will be curvaceous with gentle slopes and a slightly oblong shape. Normally the roof of a metal building will be domed. The angles made by streams or rivers that are steeply curved are associated with this element.

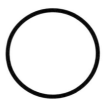

Water

A shape that is irregular is given the attribute of the water element. A water hill or building will be one that has several shapes without any regular pattern. There may even be several summits or roofs. If there are many bends in a river which do not follow a pattern, this part of the river carries the energy of the water element.

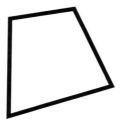

Wood

This element is used to describe a shape that is long and straight, like the trunk of a tree. A hill, mountain or building with the wood characteristics will be straight with a long body. They may be round at the top. A straight river or one that has a very wide and gentle curve will be allocated the energy of the wood element.

Fire

A shape that has sharp corners or is triangular will be given the fire element attributes. A fire building or hill will be sharp and angular. There may even be jagged pieces jutting out. The summit or roof will end with a point. Rivers or streams that have sharp and sudden changes of direction are associated with this element.

Regular shapes are always preferred to irregular shapes because they are balanced and solid and there is nothing missing from their formation .This is true for landscape, buildings, entrances, rooms, furniture, in fact everything.

If you do live in a house that has an irregular shape there are cures and enhancers that you can use to improve the level of positive Chi.

Auspicious Land Formations

The Armchair Configuration

It is most auspicious if your home or property is in a setting that gives the impression that the building is nestling in the folds of the landscape. The landscape should offer protection and support behind the building, which can be provided either by natural land formations such as a mountain or a hill, or, as will more often be the case in a modern society, the surrounding buildings. There should also be either land formations or buildings to the sides of the property, again to provide support from hostile weather conditions or attack from hostile energy fields. In front of the building there must be an open space, or, even more auspiciously, a stream or a river gently meandering by. In modern society a road will also represent the energy of a river or stream. There must not be a hill or mountain in front of the building as this will represent an obstacle to overcome.

This fortunate landscape formation is known as the 'Armchair Configuration' as it gives the impression of the property sitting in a huge, comfy armchair. People living in a property that has this auspicious landscape around the building will be able to contain the positive energy generating from the ground, while avoiding the effects of hostile Shar Chi, as they have protection. The natural build-up of the positive energy will have beneficial results regardless of the Feng Shui that they may or may not have implemented in the interior of their homes. They will avoid serious accidents or mishaps that plague people that are living without the 'Armchair Configuration' in their landscape.

For many people in a busy town or city, it is impossible to have this natural land formation. The majority of us live in built-up areas, with no control over the shapes or directions of the buildings, roads and rivers. However the beneficial effects can be recreated manually with the use of walls, hedges, fencing and even lighting in the boundaries of your property. If you are living in an area without access to a garden, do not despair, as if there are weaknesses to the exterior of your building, there are effective measures that you can take to rectify the problems inside.

The Dragon's Lair and Jade Belt

The shapes of land formations are described and symbolised in ancient Chinese texts as Celestial Animals. The most auspicious being the Dragon, the Chinese's most revered Celestial Animal. The contours of protective hills and structures are said to be the outline of the Dragon's body. To live in close vicinity to the Dragon is said to bring great good fortune.

Water has powerful symbolic value in Feng Shui, without water there would be no life. Water is the entity that supports the wood element therefore water gives life to crops that are turned into food. It is also the element that quenches thirst and is used for cleansing and purifying. The most auspicious water formation is one that curves around the front of the house or town and is known as the Jade Belt. To make the energy of the Jade Belt useful, it is important that the water is clean and fresh, it must never be allowed to become dirty or stagnant. Equally important is the speed of the flow of the water or, when using roads as rivers, the speed of the traffic. If the flow is too fast, then the Chi is moving too quickly to be harnessed and therefore will not be beneficial.

Areas that have strong and positive landscape formations are known to be auspicious as they are considered to be the Dragon's Lair. To tap into the extensive wealth of the available Feng Shui generating from this type of landscape, it is important to position the home or building comfortably inside the Dragon's Lair with the Jade Belt embracing the front of property.

The Water Dragon

Water is a powerful Feng Shui activator; it brings a life force into the environment. Water represents wealth and

Form and Landscape School

should be treated with careful consideration, as the flow of water as well as the positioning will affect this type of Chi. This is known as the Water Dragon.

Water found naturally in the landscape must always be respected. You cannot change nature but it is possible to live in harmony and tap into the boundless supply of energy that nature provides.

If there is water forming naturally around your property, note its quantity, quality and direction. To bring auspicious energy to the home, the front of the building must face this water. Water should not be seen from the back of the property nor run through the home, if this is the case, the outcome will be the reduction of stability and support. The flow of the water must be slow and gentle, if it is turbulent the Chi will be too powerful to harness, and will increase financial loss.

To bring auspicious water Chi to the home without natural resources, it is possible to create a feature that will activate this energy. There are auspicious areas for water to flourish as well as areas to avoid. The exact location of a water feature is best left to advanced Feng

Form and Landscape School

Shui formulas or a professional Feng Shui consultant. However, placing a small water feature to the left side of your front door as you stand on the threshold with your back to the property is a favoured Feng Shui tip. This will encourage money into the house. The flow of water in your water feature should be towards the property and never away from it. The water must be fresh and moving, do not allow the water to become still or stagnant, as this will encourage inauspicious yin Chi. The size of the feature should be in proportion to the area that it resides in, do not assume that a grand feature will bring bigger opportunities, as balance and harmony take precedence.

Water features can be brought into the interior of the property with the use of aquariums and pictures representing a water scene.

The Celestial Animals

There are many animals that are used in the ancient texts and scriptures of Chinese philosophy, but there are four main Celestial Animals that are used extensively throughout Feng Shui. These are the Dragon, the Tiger, the Turtle and the Phoenix. These animal terms are given to describe favourable formations in the landscape. The shape and prosperity of the land can be compared to the characteristics of these animals. It is the symbolic representation of these animals that is valuable in the Feng Shui landscape. Together these four Celestial Animals represent the auspicious landscape formation of the 'Armchair Configuration'.

The character and value of these animals is described further below:

The Dragon

Associated with the East, his colour is green and his element is wood. The Dragon is particularly important as he symbolises great good fortune and auspicious

Form and Landscape School

opportunities. In the landscape, the Dragon is represented by a hill, building or structure to the left of your building. (To find the correct position, you must stand on the threshold of your property, with your back to the interior, looking out.)

If the Dragon is missing from your landscape it is

possible to reproduce its effects by planting trees and shrubs to the left boundary of your property or by building a wall or fence. This will ensure that the energy of the Dragon is caught and harnessed, thus becoming available for fortunate Chi to pass through and around your home or office. Placing a light roughly one metre above ground level in this area will increase positive Chi.

The Tiger

Popular Feng Shui landscapes have both the Dragon and the Tiger in the landscape. While the Dragon is yang, the Tiger is yin, and therefore complements and balances the Dragon. The Tiger is associated with the west, his colour is white and his element is metal. The Tiger is represented by a hill, building or structure to the right of the property.

An important Feng Shui requirement is that the Tiger land formation should never be larger than that of the Dragon found on the left. If it is bigger, then the Feng Shui formula becomes unbalanced as the Tiger is a fierce

Form and Landscape School

creature and needs to be controlled by the majestic Dragon. If the Dragon is unable to control the changeable energy of the Tiger, conflict will result, such as disagreements with your neighbours. To reduce the impact of an excessive Tiger formation, use lights close to the ground on the right-hand side of your property.

The Turtle

The Turtle represents protection and support and is an important element in the landscape. The Turtle is associated with the north and his colour is black. The Turtle has yin energy and represents the water element. In the landscape the Turtle would be a series of buildings, hills or other structures found to the back of your property. Without a representation of the Turtle, it is as if your back is unprotected and exposed. This will place the building and the inhabitants in a vulnerable position and will encourage opportunities to slip away, as there is a lack of support.

If the representation of the Turtle is missing from your landscape, you must construct a wall or a hedge at the back of your property. If you are living in a block of flats, you can use a statue or picture of a turtle placed at the back of your property.

The Phoenix

The Phoenix is a yang entity; his energy is associated with

the south, the colour red and the fire element. The Phoenix represents fame and recognition and should be found in front of the property, represented by a small hillock. It is important that the mound of the Phoenix is not too large, otherwise the positive influence will be replaced by the energy associated with an obstacle to overcome. It is possible to reproduce the Phoenix with a bright display of red flowers at the entrance of your home.

In the 'Armchair Configuration' the Phoenix represents a footrest, with the Turtle providing the supportive back and the Dragon and Tiger representing the comfortable armrests.

Poison Arrows

Poison arrows are objects that generate unfavourable energy, Shar Chi.

If a person is living in the vicinity of a poison arrow, over a period of time they will suffer from the effects of unfavourable energy such as lack of energy, exhaustion, insomnia, sickness, conflicts, arguments and poverty. The degree of damage depends on the size of the poison arrow and how close it is to the entrance of your home. As the effects are so powerful, it is important to avoid sitting, sleeping, eating, working and living in areas that are affected by this type of energy.

The practice of Feng Shui recognises poison arrows and takes steps to either transform their effects or find ways to minimise the results. Poison Arrows are created by the presence of objects that produce intense energy or are able to cut or splinter favourable Chi.

Chi that follows long, sharp and narrow lines or objects that contain sharp angles will pick up speed until it is too fast to be of any constructive use. Chi moves around objects. If the objects are curved with soft edges, such as a plant, the Chi will flow gently, weaving in and around the leaves, and this action creates positive energy. However, if there are many straight lines in or around your home, such as telegraph poles, a long corridor or an overhanging beam, the Chi will follow the length of the straight line, gathering momentum, becoming faster and faster until it hits an obstacle. That obstacle could be you or a member of your family. Chi that is fast and furious will be difficult to harness, instead of being useful it is harmful and should be avoided.

There are several ways to avoid poison arrows, but first it is important to recognise and identify what and where they are in the landscape surrounding your house and in your home.

Exterior Poison Arrows

Offensive poison arrow structures are those with straight lines and sharp edges, such as tall tree trunks, poles, towers, electricity pylons, roads directed straight towards your front door, spiky or thorny plants, corners and roofs, in fact anything that has an aggressive or threatening appearance.

One step that can be taken to reduce the extent of a poison arrow effect is to hide or block the view from the home to the poison arrow. If you live with a tree or telegraph pole that is directly opposite and close to your entrance, you must consider blocking the view of the offending article with a hedge. If this is impossible, keeping a light on at your entrance will encourage the Chi to slow down. If you have a straight path leading to you front door, it would be better to change the path into one that is curved. This will slow the Chi into auspicious energy before it is able to enter your home.

For added protection, you could place a pair of Kirins (see page 219) opposite the poison arrow or hang a Bagua mirror (see page 195) above the entrance, which will reflect the Shar Chi back away from your home. Hanging a Bagua mirror will require careful consideration, though, as the Bagua is a very powerful Feng Shui symbol, and should never be hung inside a home.

Do keep an idea of proportion, for the poison arrow to be harmful it must be directly opposite your entrance or window and at a close distance. A telegraph pole opposite your door one mile away will not be a poison arrow, however one that is one metre away will be. The larger, sharper and more threatening the poison arrow, the more damaging the misfortune will be, as will the length of time you spend absorbing the negative energy that a poison arrow creates. It is imperative that once you have diagnosed a poison arrow, you take the necessary steps for precaution and cure. This will automatically improve the quality of Chi in your home and make cures and enhancers in the home far more effective.

The Concepts of Interior Feng Shui

Once you are satisfied that the Feng Shui that is generated from the landscape is as positive to your building as possible, and that you have taken all of the necessary steps to minimise the effects of exterior poison arrows, you are ready to move into the building.

Interior Yin and Yang

There are certain rooms in any building that will carry more yin energy than others, likewise there are some areas that will have more yang energy than others. Below is a list of typical yin and yang rooms:

Yin	Yang
Toilet, Cloakroom, Storeroom, Bedroom, Bathroom, Cupboards, Dark rooms	Kitchen, Lounge, Playroom, Study, Reception room, Office or study, Bright rooms

The Concepts of Interior Feng Shui

Colours and available natural light are natural remedies that can alter the level of yin and yang in a room, however the bedrooms, bathrooms and toilets are always considered as yin rooms. This is because bedrooms are associated with sleeping, a yin activity, bathrooms are associated with water, and toilets are associated with waste. These rooms are not used to activate Feng Shui unless there is a specific problem or reason for a cure to be placed there.

Before you begin to implement any Feng Shui cures or enhancers, walk around your rooms with a pen and paper, making lists of the yin and yang levels of energy in each room. Ask yourself:

- What colours are in the room?
- Is the furniture in proportion to the room?
- Is it comfortable to walk around in the room, or do some areas seem heavy or cluttered?
- How many electrical items are there in the room?
- Is this room dull and dark or stimulating and bright?
- Does it smell musty or is the air fresh?
- Is there a balance between light and dark furnishings and colours?

This will give you a very good indication of what energy is already available to you and what energy you have been living with. As you begin to make changes, the energy will shift and areas that may have accumulated high levels of yin Chi can be altered until there is a healthy balance between yin and yang.

Rooms that are naturally yin, such as bedrooms, should be kept calm, as if you paint them in bright, vibrant colours, such as red or yellow, you will risk disturbing your sleep. Yin energy should be left in the appropriate places, undisturbed, whereas yang rooms will respond to stimulation, and will reap the expected rewards. Therefore, concentrate on the rooms that are yang in nature, which are the activity rooms.

Ideally yin rooms should be kept at a distance from the main entrance to the home or office, with the yang active rooms kept at the front of the building.

Interior Poison Arrows

Poison arrows that are found in the home will have the same energy effect as exterior poison arrows.

Interior poison arrows can be found in overhead beams, corners from cabinets, long corridors, the backs of books in an exposed bookcase, in fact anything that has sharp angles directed at you whilst you are sleeping, eating, sitting or working.

Interior poison arrows can be addressed more easily than exterior ones, as it is possible to disguise them or move away from their offending effects without construction work to the building. If you do suffer from interior poison arrows there are several cures that you could use:

- Soften the sharp angles from an overhead beam with drapes or material.
- Move your bed or chair away from the offending angle.
- Place an object such as a plant or statue in front of the poison arrow.

- Place spotlights under a beam with the light directed upwards.
- Build a false ceiling to hide overhead beams.
- Place doors on bookshelves, so that they become cupboards.
- Hang a pair of flutes at either end of a beam with the mouthpieces touching the wall so that the energy is directed up rather than downward.

Interior Support – the 'Armchair Configuration'

If you spend periods of time sitting down in your home or office, you should follow the rules for the 'Armchair Configuration' (see page 65).

In a yang room such as an office, lounge or study, sit where there is always support behind you, never sit with your back exposed to an empty open space, window or door. There should be representations of the Turtle, Dragon and Tiger in their appropriate places as well as an open space in front of you. For an auspicious arrangement, include an image of water such as a waterfall in front of where you sit, but never behind it. This will be symbolic of wealth coming towards you, rather than leaving you behind. To increase the energy associated with support, place an image of a mountain behind you. You could also use a statue or image of a Turtle, which is a powerful symbolic Celestial Animal.

For the bedroom, a yin room, this rule will be important for the positioning of the bed. Always place the bed against a solid wall, never underneath a window. To increase and maintain regular support, it is recommended that you use a solid headboard.

Blast from the Door

'Blast from the Door' is the effect created by Chi that is moving too fast to be useful as it enters a room. It is important not to be the first obstacle the Chi encounters.

The 'Blast from the Door' will cause a person to become anxious when they sit with their back to an open door. It is uncomfortable, as to see who is behind them they must look over their shoulder. Subconsciously, a person will feel uncomfortable sitting or sleeping in this position. For protection purposes, it is advisable to sit or sleep in an area of the room where your body is not exposed to the entrance. The best position would in a part of the room where you have a solid wall behind you for support and an open space in front of you. You should be able to glance up and see the door comfortably from your sitting position and have plenty of room for freedom of movement.

This rule is particularly important if the Chi has been able to gather momentum, for example from travelling through a long corridor without encountering obstacles.

Windows must be included in this rule as well as doors, as Chi is able to leave and enter a room through the glass.

Declining Support

This is a practical rule; it is inadvisable for a person to sit in the corner of the room with their desk or bed positioned at an angle. This is due to the symbolic value of the two walls joining together; it will be as if your support is declining. Chi will also collect in corners and if the Chi stays still for too long it will become stagnant and cause damage to your wellbeing. Corners are perfect places to place active objects, such as telephones, facsimile machines, televisions, clocks, radios and lights, as the yang energy that they generate will keep the Chi moving.

Mirrors

Mirrors have high value as simple and effective Feng Shui enhancers and cures. The power of mirrors stems from their reflective surfaces and they become very versatile tools. They can be used to double positive images. Hanging a mirror over a dining table will double the value of the food and family harmony it reflects. However, mirrors should not be hung where they are reflect a poison arrow, toilet, staircase or any negative image as they will double the Chi of the negative image.

Mirrors can be used in dark areas that require light and you can position a mirror so that light is bounced into a space that would otherwise remain dark and still. They can also be used to increase the illusion of space.

When using a mirror it is important that the image you are reflecting is positive and whole; do not allow the image to become split or fractionated. Glass that has joints or breaks, such as mirrored tiles or mirror mosaics, will split the image into different pieces, therefore creating a confusion of Chi, and this will be unhelpful for Feng Shui requirements. When hanging a mirror to reflect your own body, have a mirror that is as large as possible to reflect all of your body, never have part of your head, neck or shoulders chopped off.

It is not recommended to hang mirrors in the bedroom, especially opposite the bed, as this will alter the quality of sleep. The Chi will continue to bounce back and forth from you to the mirror all night long. How tiring!

Mirrors hung in the hallway will give the impression of space and light, which is deemed auspicious. It is advisable to hang a mirror to the side of the door but mirrors should never be hung opposite the door as the

The Concepts of Interior Feng Shui

Chi entering the building will be reflected straight back outside.

Locations

The positioning and location of rooms in your space is a major Feng Shui consideration. There will be parts of your home or office that will contain more yang active and positive energy while other areas will have a natural amount of yin energy. It is important to have active rooms placed where the Chi is naturally in tune with your desired atmosphere, and keep yin rooms to the quieter areas of the building.

The Dragon's Gate

The 'Dragon's Gate' is the term given to the main entrance of your home or business. Perhaps the most important part of your building, the main entrance is where you pass through every day, and is also the main point of entrance for the Chi that will affect you and your home or office. It is must therefore be treated with respect.

The direction the door faces is also important as it gives an indication of what type of Chi is crossing over the threshold of your property.

If the front door and path leading to the main door are dirty and neglected, they will collect negative levels of Chi, which will pass through the doorway and into your home.

The main entrance of your home or office is one of the first impressions that people will use to gather information about you. If the entrance access is strewn with obstacles or is long and narrow, visitors will form an opinion of you as an uncaring and perhaps difficult person. This will place you at a disadvantage before you have even met them.

It is of crucial value, therefore, that the front and entrance of your home is as attractive, spacious and bright as possible to encourage a warm and friendly welcome. This type of energy moving in and around your home will provide an auspicious environment. Ideally, keep a light on above or next to the front door and have healthy plants nearby. A small hanging basket of cascading plants will generate positive energy that will affect the whole building.

The Concepts of Interior Feng Shui

The entrance should be as large and as uncluttered as possible to maximise the level of Chi entering your home. The hallway should be kept as bright, attractive and inviting as possible, which will give the Chi support as it embarks on its journey through your home or business. If your door opens to a poison arrow it is important that you take steps to reduce the negative influence as much as possible.

The Three Door Effect

A very important Feng Shui requirement to maximise Chi to its full potential, is to capture as much Sheng Chi (positive energy) as possible and reduce the risk of Chi escaping or leaking away before it has been properly utilised. The most common problem is known as the 'Three Door' effect, where the front door and back door to the property are actually opposite each other, often with a third opening in the same line. This will actually encourage Chi to rush from the front entrance straight through the building, and out through the back door, before it has not been given the chance to circulate through the rest of the property. If the 'Three Door' effect is combined with a long corridor the outcome is even more disastrous as the Chi will gather speed and momentum, becoming fast and furious as it passes through your building.

To reduce this effect, you must always keep at least one of the doors closed to prevent Chi from escaping, and encourage it to move to other areas of your home instead. You could place a wind chime near the entrance, which will disperse Chi. A light kept on at the front door will slow active Chi before it enters your home or office.

To slow Chi down in a long corridor, add objects such as plants, furniture and statues along the length of the corridor. The Chi will meander gently around each object. If the corridor is too narrow for objects to be placed on the ground, use the ceiling, hanging wind chimes or banners. You could also use atmospheric lighting, bright colourful pictures and mirrors to make the area more interesting. Light colours on the wall will increase the illusion of space.

The Concepts of Interior Feng Shui

The Lounge or Living Room

This room is normally the main room in the house that is used by all the family, it is a yang room, and there will be higher levels of yang energy in this room than in any other room, with the exception of the kitchen. It is in this room that the family will gather together and it is also a social room for entertaining guests. This room will normally have electrical items, such as a television, video, music player, or perhaps an aquarium, all of which encourage the generation of more yang energy.

As this is the room where the majority of the family will spend most time other than when they are sleeping, it is important that the energy is productive and satisfying, rather than unbalanced and draining. This is the room that will most affect the moods and emotions of the inhabitants.

If possible, use the behaviour of children to gauge the level of yin and yang energy in this room; children are extremely sensitive to energy fields as they have not mastered the art of self-control. If it the room is over-stimulating with too much yang energy, children will become hyperactive. If the room has too much yin energy, children will become lethargic and easily bored.

The best location for this room is as close to the main entrance as possible; this will enable the Chi entering the building to pass into this room first.

Reduce the risk of escaping or leaking Chi by covering your windows with opaque glass, net curtains, shutters or blinds. Cover the windows with curtains in the evening to prevent yin energy from entering through the windows.

Keep ample space between the furniture to enable Chi to travel freely.

Do not sit in front of the doorway, or with your back exposed to either a window or door to avoid the 'Blast from the Door' effect. Do not sit directly in line with a poison arrow. If there is a poison arrow in the room, either move your seat to another position or take steps to rectify the poison arrow effect.

Use colours that are warm and inviting, such as shades of yellow, which is an auspicious colour as it associated with warmth, cosiness and gathering together. If you have dark or heavy furniture, use pale colours on the walls and soft furnishings to create a balance.

The Dining Room or Conference Room

The room where the family sit together during meal times will be a yang room. It offers the opportunity for communication and family harmony and should be treated with respect and importance. Ideally this room should be placed near the main entrance to enable positive Chi to enter whilst it is still strong. The room should be kept as bright and cheerful as possible. It would be auspicious to have photos of the family and relations in this room.

The same rules apply to an office conference room, where it would be auspicious to have photos of your members of staff to promote team spirit.

The dining table or conference table should be situated in a part of the room where there is plenty of access so that the Chi can circulate freely. The most auspicious shape for the table is round or oval as this eliminates the possibility of poison arrows and encourages the Chi to follow the curves without leaving at any angles. Communication will flow easily, as the energy continually revolves around the table.

Do not position the dining table in a room that is situated beneath a toilet, as the energy associated with waste will disturb the atmosphere and taint the energy of the food.

A popular Feng Shui enhancer to double the Chi for nutrition and family harmony is to hang a mirror in a position where it reflects the table, the people and the food. Food is symbolic of wealth and prosperity; to make the experience as beneficial as possible, encourage family harmony at mealtimes.

The Concepts of Interior Feng Shui

The Study or Office

The level of activity in a study or office will have a bearing on its levels of yin and yang energy. If the room is intended to house a busy business, then you need to make sure it is given a yang energy emphasis. This will stimulate the mind and encourage a busy atmosphere. If, however, the room is intended to be used as a quiet retreat, then the décor and energy will need to reflect the yin aspect to encourage peace and receptivity.

The positioning of the desk is of prime importance. Following the 'Armchair Configuration', you should sit comfortably with support behind you and an open space in front of you. To give extra Feng Shui support, you could place a picture of a mountain or a statue of a turtle behind you. Another auspicious Feng Shui tip is to place an aquarium or a picture of moving water in front of your desk, as this will encourage wealth and prosperity to flow towards you. It is imperative that the picture shows the flow of water moving towards you rather than away.

To avoid suffering from the effects of 'Blast from the Door' do not place the desk in line with the door.

Identify and remedy any poison arrows, the most important being those that will affect you as you sit at your desk.

Bedrooms

Spending time in a bedroom which has positive Feng Shui will immediately improve your quality of sleep, promote good health and increase romantic happiness for couples. Bedrooms are yin rooms as the energy that is associated with the bedroom is normally restful sleep and peacefulness. If you are sharing a bedroom then another consideration is human harmony.

It is important that a bedroom has quiet energy, therefore it is inadvisable to place this room above or below a noisy active room, such as an office, shop or lounge. Nor should you keep active objects such as a television, sound system or aquarium in the bedroom.

Use colours that are gentle and relaxing. Soft pastel shades are recommended, as are colour washes. Avoid bright and vibrant block colours and never position a mirror opposite the bed.

Watch out for poison arrows that may cut into your energy whilst you are sleeping, and position the bed away from the door to avoid the problems associated with the 'Blast from the Door' effect. If it is impossible to move the bed, cover poison arrows with material or hide them behind a screen. A screen will also be an effective cure from the 'Blast from the Door'.

To give yourself support while you are sleeping, position the bed so that it has solid support from the wall. Do not place your bed underneath a window or at an angle. A headboard will give extra support and comfort and is therefore recommended for Feng Shui purposes.

It is recommended for couples sleeping in the same room to sleep in a double bed rather than two separate beds. This will give support to the relationship, while two separate beds are symbolic of separation.

Do not sleep underneath a shelf or cupboard, this will act as a poison arrow putting extra pressure on your head and have a negative effect on your health and sleep pattern.

The Bathroom and Toilet

Toilets receive plenty of 'bad press' in Feng Shui because of their association with the collection of waste.

For Feng Shui purposes the positioning of toilet and bathrooms are very important. If the toilet is in a part of your house that is associated with your wealth or romantic happiness, then symbolically the toilet will flush away all of the Chi associated with these energies. Not only that, but every time you pass close to a toilet or bathroom, you are reminded of the waste association, which could disturb your focus on other more important or positive thought patterns. It is therefore recommended that you keep the lid of the toilet down to prevent Chi from moving in and around the toilet bowl. Even better would be to keep the door of the bathroom or toilet closed at all times as 'out of sight is out of mind'.

However, toilets that are positioned in yin areas of the home or business will be auspicious as they will flush away all of your negative energy. This rule applies to store rooms, garages and bathrooms.

The Concepts of Interior Feng Shui

Toilets should never be placed above the entrance to your home, kitchen, bedroom or dining room, to avoid the possibility of Chi becoming spoilt.

If the toilet has become a Feng Shui problem area, then there are ways to reduce the level of disturbance that it creates. First if possible use another toilet, otherwise keep the toilet door closed at all times. For lighting, use an uplighter that will encourage the Chi to rise upwards, and keep the area outside of the toilet bright and cheerful to improve the Chi. In severe cases, a five-bar wind chime can be hung outside the inauspicious room to disperse the negative implications.

The Staircase

The shape and position of your staircase must be given consideration, as it will have the power to alter the Chi as it passes from floor to floor. If the staircase is straight, the Chi will move far more quickly than if it were curved. A curved staircase is seen as more auspicious as Chi will move up it in a gentle, swirling movement. The steps of the stairs should always be solid, otherwise Chi will pass through the stairs, resulting in a leakage of Chi.

The best location for the stairs is in a quiet, non-active part of the house, such as the back of the building. It is preferable to have the new energy passing through the building, circulating fully in the active rooms before passing onto another level and stairs that are directly opposite the front door will encourage Chi to escape before it has been given the chance to circulate properly.

To reduce the possibility of Chi moving too quickly via the stairs, hang a wind chime above the staircase to disperse a level of Chi. A light left on over the stairs will also encourage Chi to slow down. If your front door opens to face the stairs, you could move the hinges to the opposite side of the doorframe to prevent the door opening straight onto the stairs.

The Concepts of Interior Feng Shui

The Kitchen

The kitchen houses two powerful objects with opposing elements: the oven or hob which belongs to the fire element and the sink (and possibly dishwasher) which belongs to the water element. The water and fire elements oppose one another so it is not recommended that these two appliances be placed next to each other. If they are, their combining energy fields will cause disruption and chaos to your kitchen. Bearing in mind that this is the room where your food is prepared and cooked, it is important that it is kept in harmony to avoid negative Chi affecting your meals.

Another consideration is the positioning of the oven, which is known as 'The Dragon's Mouth'. Here you should follow the same rules as for the bed in the bedroom. In other words, follow the 'Armchair Configuration', providing a solid wall for support and do not place the oven beneath a window or at an angle. The oven should not be seen from the door, so as to avoid the 'Blast from the Door' problem.

Avoid poison arrows, especially those that are directed at you whilst you are preparing food or spending time at the sink, as your back will be exposed and unprotected.

The Theory of the Compass School

The Compass School is the next level of Feng Shui that you can apply to your home once you have familiarised yourself with the Form or Landscape School. It is worth bearing in mind that the Compass School can be implemented by itself without support from the Form School, however the results will be more noticeable and rewarding if the landscape Feng Shui is favourable to you.

There are several components that make up the Compass School and that take into account your date of birth and the door directions, space and locations of rooms in your house.

The main principal behind the Compass School is the eight different variations of Chi that emanate from the eight directions of a compass. There are four cardinal directions – north, south, west and east, and four sub-directions – northeast, northwest, southeast and southwest. Each direction has an associated 'type' of energy. The theory originated from ancient formulas based on calculations made from the I Ching and the Bagua. Both the I Ching and the Bagua are based on arrangements of trigrams.

Trigrams

The trigrams were invented roughly 4000 years ago by the Chinese ruler Fu Hsi, to show symbolically the meaning of opposites relating to heaven and earth. Each trigram consists of three layers of lines that are either broken or unbroken. A broken line represents yin energy, an unbroken line represents yang energy. There are eight trigrams and each one is associated with a particular form of natural phenomenon. These are:

Heaven	☰	Wind	☴
Water	☵	Thunder	☳
Earth	☷	Mountain	☶
Fire	☲	Lake	☱

The Theory of the Compass School

The trigrams are arranged in sequence. There are two forms of trigram sequences. The first arrangement by Fu Hsi, is known as the Early Heaven Sequence, The second, the Later Heaven Sequence, was arranged by King Wen, who wanted to apply the trigrams to man's existence on earth. This second arrangement is known as the Later Heaven Sequence.

I Ching

The I Ching is a classical Chinese book that is perhaps the oldest book in existence. Another name for the I Ching is The Book of Changes. It is a book that has evolved over approximately 5,000 years and has been influenced by many religions and philosophies. One of its uses is for divination, another is as a source of the wisdom behind the Compass School formula of Feng Shui.

The I Ching is based on the patterns and cycles of the heavens, the earth, nature and the seasons and the effect that they have on man. It is the interpretation of sixty-four hexagrams that holds the key to a wealth of information in the I Ching. Each hexagram is a combination of two trigrams. Each of the eight trigrams represents a compass direction, among other attributes.

Bagua

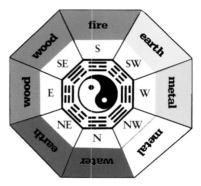

The Bagua is an eight-sided symbol that is used for one of the formulas in the Compass School. The translation of Bagua is 'eight numbers'.

There is a spiritual aspect to the Bagua based on the

The Theory of the Compass School

positioning of eight trigrams that are the codes behind Feng Shui. It is these trigrams in their special formula which make the Bagua a powerful and protective symbol. The Bagua symbol can be placed outside the home to protect the inhabitants from harm induced by evil spirits or poison arrows.

The Bagua is separated into eight sectors; each section associated with a number, an element, a compass direction and an energy aspiration. The Bagua is the tool used for the 'Eight Aspirations' formula.

There are other attributes for each direction, which are used in more advanced levels of Feng Shui and require the wisdom and experience of professional Feng Shui Masters using a Lo-Pan Compass.

Notice the arrangement of trigrams in the centre of the Bagua. This arrangement, the Later Heaven Sequence, is used for Feng Shui positioning.

Lo-Shu

The ancient Chinese recognised the power of mathematics and the patterns produced by numbers, in fact they believed that everything in life and the universe could be explained in numerical terms. Therefore they have great respect for and make emphasis on the value and sequences of numbers. The most powerful sequence of numbers is known as the 'Lo Shu Square'.

The positioning of numbers in the Lo Shu is unique. Add up the numbers on any line in the square, horizontal, vertically or diagonal, and the answer will always be fifteen. Another name for the Lo Shu is the 'magic

The Theory of the Compass School

square'. In ancient Chinese texts this sequence of numbers is said to have magic properties, and is used in powerful Feng Shui formulas.

Over thousands of years, the Lo Shu and the Bagua formulas evolved and became entwined to contribute to the Compass School. When these formulas are used in conjunction with an accurate floor plan of your home, they are extremely potent for Feng Shui purposes. It is the Lo Shu that will give numerical value to the cures and enhancers that you use in your Feng Shui.

Practical Use of the Compass School Formulas

Pen and Paper, Compass, Floor Plan

The first step in Feng Shui is detailed preparation. Take your time, if you are too impatient and start activating sectors of your home or business without careful forethought or knowledge, you will be gambling with the expected results.

When you are implementing energy to enhance your luck, you must be focused and firm with your intentions, otherwise you risk making a mistake and encouraging the wrong type of energy that may activate or antagonise a problem that you want to avoid. Therefore, one of the most powerful tools will be you, and putting pen to paper.

Start from outside your home, by standing on your doorstep and writing down all of the distinguishing features that are immediately in your surroundings. Include drains, trees, roads, other buildings, hedges,

Practical Use of the Compass School Formula

lights, water features, hills and anything that could represent a poison arrow. Then listen to the sounds, make a note of the noise levels. Are you in a yang scenario where you are positioned in or near a busy street, heavy traffic or perhaps a railway station or airport? Or is the Chi more yin in nature? Do you live in a quiet cul-de-sac or in the middle of the country? How close are your neighbours? Next, look for the 'Armchair Configuration' and look for structures or natural formations that could represent the Dragon, Tiger, Turtle and Phoenix. Are they all present or will some need to be reconstructed?

Once you have gained enough information to judge the quality of Chi in and around your building, you are able to take the next step, which is to measure the compass directions, starting from your main entrance. The next stage is to apply this information to the floor plan of your home. You can then compare it to the Feng Shui rules and formulas and begin to make adjustments.

How to Read a Compass

When taking compass measurements for the first time, you should choose a compass that is simple and easy to read. Do not be tempted into buying a Lo Pan or extremely sensitive compass as they will only confuse you. These days you can also buy an electronic compass which will give you accurate readings at a push of a button.

First, stand facing the direction that you would like to measure. For example, if you stand on your doorstep facing the outside, you will be measuring the direction that your door is facing. The compass needle will spin and move as it searches for magnetic north.

Take at least three readings, the first from your doorstep, the second at least a metre away and the third a metre further away. This is necessary as compass reading can be altered by other magnetic forces, such as overhead and underground cables, geopathic stress or underground drains or streams. Even cars and people will generate enough energy to affect your compass readings. Use the average of all three readings to find the direction of north.

Once you know which direction north is, you can mark it down on your floor plan. Now you will be able to work out south, east and west and the sub-directions by drawing dividing lines across your floor plan.

Breaking a Floor Plan into Feng Shui Sectors

To apply accurate Feng Shui using the Compass School, you will need to take careful measurements of your home and transform them into a reliable floor plan that is accurate and to scale. In scale with the plan, place all major features, including the doors, large pieces of furniture and the stairs. Include as much information as possible.

Once you have your measurements and have drawn up your floor plan, you must find where the physical centre of your home is and mark out the directions. To do this, follow these steps:

- First, stand on your doorstep with your back to your building, point the compass and measure that direction. Remember, the needle will point to magnetic north, so mark the north direction onto your floor plan.

- Draw a circle around your plan and mark faintly a line from the point on your map that represents north to the opposite side of the circle. This will represent the north to south axis.

- Place a protractor on this line and mark the point at ninety degrees from the line on your circle. Draw a line from this point to the opposite side of the circle, crossing the north–south axis. This is the east to west axis. You should now have four equal sections over your plan.

- Next, divide the circle into eight equal sections by drawing two further lines across the centre. These represent the northwest to southeast and southwest to northeast axes. Each section should be exactly the same size, taking up forty-five degrees of the circle. Your floor plan should now have eight different

Practical Use of the Compass School Formula

sections, all with their relative direction, to be used later with the Bagua and the Eight Aspirations formula.

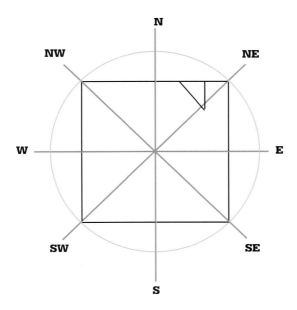

Next place a grid over your floor plan that is made of nine equal size boxes; this will be useful at a later stage for dividing the floor plan into favourable and unfavourable sectors, according to the Eight Mansions formula.

NW	N	NE
W		E
SW	S	SE

Irregular Floor Plans

The best Feng Shui results come from an area that has solid and regular features, such as a square. Not all house or buildings are built with this kind of design; in fact modern architects pride themselves on inventive and ingenious ways to make each building as unique and individual as possible. If your floor plan is an irregular shape, there will be some additional steps that you will need to take before implementing any cures or enhancers.

Two Grids

An area that is irregular will need to be treated either as two separate areas or as an area that has a missing corner. If the size of the missing corner is very large, then it is better to draw two grids, one for each section. Treat the Feng Shui of each section separately.

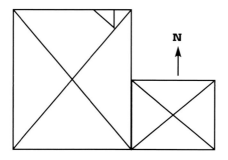

Missing Corner

If your floor plan has a small missing corner, you could treat the missing corner with Feng Shui enhancers to rectify the problem. Place a light outside at the point where the corner should be to increase yang energy. Alternatively place an object such as a statue or heavy stone at that point to provide grounding for the area.

If you do not have access to the outside then you will have to place a cure on the inside. One cure would be to place a mirror on the wall that has the missing corner. The mirror will reflect the image of the room and increase the idea of space.

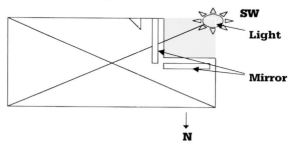

SW

Light

Mirror

N

Practical Use of the Compass School Formula

You can also address the missing energy with objects following the Constructive Cycle of elements, depending on which sector of the Bagua the missing corner is in. For example, the southwest is the sector on the Bagua that represents marriage and romantic happiness, so if this is where the missing corner is, it could negatively affect those aspects of your life. To reinforce this energy, you must increase the element that is associated with that direction. The element that is related to the southwest is earth, therefore it would be auspicious to hang crystal pendants from the window or place a pair of ceramic statues in this area. Fire is the element that supports the earth, so it would be auspicious to light candles or a table lamp is this area. Using the colours pink to red will increase yang Chi associated with romance.

Looking at the Destructive Cycle it is possible to see that the wood element has the power to weaken the earth further, and so it is advisable to avoid placing plants in such an area.

The Eight Mansion Formula

The Eight Mansion Formula is a very effective formula, though it is not always possible to implement all of the best directions for every person, all of the time, especially when there is more than one person living or working in the same place. For this reason it is advisable to concentrate on the head of the family or team, as he or she is providing for the family as a whole.

The Eight Mansion Formula is based on compass directions and a time dimension. Each person has four favourable and four unfavourable directions, each one associated with a particular type of energy. The favourable directions will affect you positively every time you are standing, sitting or sleeping facing them. Likewise the four unfortunate directions will have a negative influence on you every time you are standing, sitting or sleeping facing them.

This rule will apply to your front entrance. If your entrance is in a direction that is favourable to you then that energy will be available to you at all times. If however your door opens onto an unfavourable direction, you must take steps to disperse the energy using the five elements Destructive Cycle.

There is a simple formula you can use to determine which are your favourable and which are your unfavourable directions. It is based on the year that you were born. By following the formulas, one for women and one for men, you will find your 'Kua' number. Each Kua number has four fortunate directions and four inauspicious directions.

The Kua Formulas

The Chinese years are slightly different from those of the western calendar, since they begin the New Year in the first few days of February. If your birthday falls into the period between the end of January and the middle of February, you will have to double-check which year your birthday falls into.

For His Kua Number:

- Take the last two digits from his year of birth and add them together
- If you are left with two numbers add them together until you are left with one number
- Take this number and deduct it from ten
- The resulting number will be his Kua number

For Her Kua number:

- Take the last two digits from her year of birth and add them together
- Add the numbers again if necessary until you are left with one number under ten
- Take this number and add five
- If you are left with double digits, add the two numbers together until you are left with one digit
- This number will be her Kua number

The Eight Mansion Formula

East House or West House

Your Kua number will determine whether you fall into one of two groups, East House and West House. People who have a Kua number that is part of the East House will find that they will be particularly sensitive to the elements of water, wood and fire, and so these elements are favourable for Feng Shui purposes. Those who have a Kua number that falls into the West House category will be sensitive to the earth and metal elements, and will find materials such as stones, crystal and wind chimes very effective.

East House Kua Numbers and Auspicious Directions

Energy Associated With:	Kua Number 1 Directions	Kua Number 3 Directions
Success	Southeast	South
Health	East	North
Relationships	South	Southeast
Spirituality	North	East

Energy associated with:	Kua Number 4 Directions	Kua Number 9 Directions
Success	North	East
Health	South	Southeast
Relationships	East	North
Spirituality	Southeast	South

West House Kua Numbers and Auspicious Directions

Energy Associated With:	Kua Number 2 Directions	Kua Number 5 female Directions
Success	Northeast	Southwest
Health	West	Northwest
Relationships	Northwest	West
Spirituality	Southwest	Northeast

The Eight Mansion Formula

Energy Associated With:	Kua Number 5 male Directions	Kua Number 8 Directions
Success	Northeast	Southwest
Health	West	Northwest
Relationships	Northwest	West
Spirituality	Southwest	Northeast

Energy Associated With:	Kua Number 6 Directions	Kua Number 7 Directions
Success	West	Northwest
Health	Northeast	Southwest
Relationships	Southwest	Northeast
Spirituality	Northwest	West

Favourable Directions and Applications

From your Kua number you will have found four auspicious directions and the energy associated with each direction. Their meanings and applications are:

Success Direction

This has a Feng Shui term of 'Sheng Chi' and it means that whenever you are facing this direction, in the office and at home, you will be facing the Chi associated with opportunities for success and great wealth. Your mind will be focused and concentrated, you will act with clarity and confidence. You should face this direction whenever possible.

Health Direction

The Feng Shui term for this direction is 'Tien Yi' and it represents comfortable living and wealth opportunities. It offers support from family and friends and promotes good health. It would be favourable to place your bed so that your head points in this direction when you sleep.

Relationship Direction

The Feng Shui term for this direction is 'Nien Yen' and it will encourage harmony between the family, friends and colleagues. This direction will also support romance and the opportunity for marriage and support a stable income. By sleeping or spending time facing this direction you will absorb this energy.

Spirituality Direction

The Feng Shui term for this direction is 'Fu Wei'. Here the emphasis is not on material wealth, instead it is a direction which will strengthen you spiritually. It is associated with a favourable and contented life, without spectacular wealth but with happiness. This will be a favourable direction to study or meditate in, as you will receive the energy connected to inner peace and receptivity.

Avoidable Directions and Circumstances

The four favourable and affluent directions are balanced by four unfavourable directions. These four directions each carry a negative meaning. The depth of misfortune depends on the direction you are facing. It is important to avoid facing, sitting, eating or sleeping in any of these directions.

East House Kua Numbers – Unfavourable Directions

Energy Associated With:	Kua Number 1 Directions	Kua Number 3 Directions
Accidents and Mishaps	West	Southwest
Five Ghosts	Northeast	Northwest
Six Killings	Northwest	Northeast
Total Loss	Southwest	West

The Eight Mansion Formula

Energy Associated With:	Kua Number 4 Directions	Kua Number 9 Directions
Accidents and Mishaps	Northwest	Northeast
Five Ghosts	Southwest	West
Six Killings	West	Southwest
Total Loss	Northeast	Northwest

West House Kua Numbers – Unfavourable Directions

Energy Associated With:	Kua Number 2 Directions	Kua Number 5 female Directions
Accidents and Mishaps	East	South
Five Ghosts	Southeast	North
Six Killings	South	East
Total Loss	North	Southeast

Energy Associated with:	Kua Number 5 male Directions	Kua Number 8 Directions
Accidents and Mishaps	East	South
Five Ghosts	Southeast	North
Six Killings	South	East
Total Loss	North	Southeast

Energy associated with:	Kua Number 6 male Directions	Kua Number 7 Directions
Accidents and Mishaps	Southeast	North
Five Ghosts	East	South
Six Killings	North	Southeast
Total Loss	South	East

The Eight Mansion Formula

As with the favourable directions, each inauspicious direction has a title and a meaning. These are:

Accidents and Mishaps

The Feng Shui term for this energy is 'Ho Hai'. As the title sounds, this direction is associated will minor accidents and mishaps to general day-to-day living. It will be an unlucky direction to spend time in or to face, eat or sleep in.

Five Ghosts

The Feng Shui term for this direction is 'Wu Kwai'. This energy is associated with fires and loss of belongings, such as a burglary. The implications of this direction are worse than that of 'Ho Hai'. You should avoid this direction whenever possible.

Six Killings

The Feng Shui name for this energy is 'Lui Sha'. This energy is even more serious than the first two. It will affect your health, and cause relationships with others, including your family, to become strained. It will cause obstacles and troubles in your professional life, with others taking promotions that pass you by. Avoid facing, sitting, eating or sleeping in this direction at all times.

Total Loss

The Feng Shui term for this direction is 'Chueh Ming'. It is by far the worst direction and will bring misfortune to you, your family and business, causing you to suffer extreme hardships and personal loss. Not only must you avoid spending time in this direction, but you must also ensure that your home, or the opening of the main entrance, does not face this direction. If they do, you must take steps to change things as you do not want to encourage this energy entering your home and affecting all of the cures and enhancers that are in place.

The Eight Aspirations Formula

There are two main requirements for this formula, one is the Bagua and the other is for you to know your intention, or what area of your life you wish to improve. The formula has evolved from the I Ching, the Bagua and the Lo Shu. To activate this formula you will need a floor plan of your home or office including compass directions, representatives of the five elements (wood, fire, earth, metal and water) for cures and enhancers and an image of the Bagua, which will be used as a template.

This formula should only be used in rooms that have yang energy. Do not use it in rooms such as the toilet, bathroom, bedroom, garage and storeroom. These are yin rooms and will carry negative implications. In those rooms you can use the Destructive Cycle of elements to 'press down' the negative energy.

Each section of the Bagua is labelled with a compass direction, an element and an aspiration. For this formula to work, you must divide your floor plan into eight sections (see page 119) and label each section with the correct compass direction. Using the image of the Bagua as a template, lay it over your floor plan, you should now be able to give each section an aspiration and element.

Aspiration Sections of the Bagua

South – Fame and Recognition

This is a fire sector, it will be supported by wood and more fire, therefore use the colours red and/or green. Lights and plants will bring support, as will statutes of horses. The number nine is auspicious here.

Southwest – Romance and Marriage Harmony

This is an earth sector; fire and earth will support it. The colours red, pink and purple will represent the fire element, yellows through to brown will represent the earth element. Fire objects include lamps and candles; earth objects include ceramics, crystals and stoneware. Rose Quartz would be a recommended stone to use in this area as an enhancer. The number two represents this sector, so to have a pair of statues representing a couple will be auspicious here.

West – Children and Projects

This is a metal sector and will be supported by the earth and metal elements. Earthy colours and metallic colours will be suitable in this area, as will the colour white which is another metal colour. Clocks and other metallic objects will be supportive in this sector. The number seven represents this sector. Children would benefit from studying or completing homework in this sector.

Northwest – Networking

This is another metal sector so the requirements are the same as for the west sector. Computers and telephones are auspicious here. Six is the number for this section. This area holds positive energy for communication. It would be auspicious to keep pictures of your friends and family in metal frames in this sector.

North – Career

This sector is represented by the water element, therefore to increase the energy associated with job prospects, career development and promotion you will need to increase the metal and water elements in this sector. The colours blue and black represent the water element. A water feature will be auspicious, provided that the water is kept clean and moving. Make sure that the flow of water is towards you rather than away. Water scenes will bring good fortune, as will an aquarium. Metallic objects or circular objects will bring support. The number one represents this sector.

Northeast – Education and Spirituality

The northeast is an earth sector; it will be supported by the fire and earth elements. The number eight represents it. A painting of a mountain will bring support and security when placed in this area. This will be a positive area to have a study or office, as the energy is associated with focus and concentration. You could keep religious statues and artefacts in this area, and meditation will have far-reaching results here.

East – Health and Travel

This is a wood sector and will be supported by the water and wood elements. This area should be kept clean and bright. The colours that support this energy will be bright blues and greens. The air should be kept fresh; flowers and healthy pot plants symbolic of positive health would be auspicious here. A globe in this area would stimulate the energy associated with travel, especially if you were able to spin it every time you walked past or if it had a light inside, which you could keep on at all times.

Southeast – Wealth and Prosperity

This is another wood sector so water and wood are the elements to focus on. A water feature would be auspicious; you could place an aquarium or painting of a waterfall here to represent opportunities coming to you. Healthy plants in this area will be symbolic of financial growth.

Southeast is represented by the wood element, specifically yin wood. For Feng Shui purposes it would be important to have this area as yang as possible and as large as possible, to increase positive wealth and prosperity energy. If are applying this formula to your office, this would be a positive room for sales. Active objects will stimulate yang energy; therefore lights, televisions, telephones and computers will be beneficial in this room.

Using The Five Elements As Cures and Enhancers

To activate the aspirations on the Bagua you will need to use the five elements in the Constructive Cycle. By increasing the elemental energy you are making the opportunities bigger and stronger, you will also be increasing your confirmations and every time you spend time in this space there will be a constant reminder of your aspirations.

If you have a negative room, such as a toilet, in an important sector, you will need Feng Shui to suppress the negative outcome, by using the sequence of elements as shown in the Destructive Cycle.

For example, if the southeast part of your home contained the toilet, there will be a negative influence on this energy. You will need to decrease this energy, as it is associated with money running away. As the southeast is a wood element, you must press down on the wood. Using the Destructive Cycle of elements, you know that metal and fire will weaken the wood. By hanging a small wind chime near the doorway to disperse the energy and using upward lights to force the energy upwards and away from the toilet, you will drastically reduce the negative implications. You may then use the Bagua on a yang room such as the lounge and activate the southeast sector of that room to rectify the toilet problem.

Using Colours as Cures

The following table shows each of the elements and their relationship with one and another and how to use colours to control them.

	Earth
Supported by:	Fire
Colours to use:	Red/Pink/Purple
Controlling:	Water
Colours to use:	Black/Navy Blue
Exhausted by:	Metal
Colours to use:	White/Metallic colours
Destroyed by:	Wood
Colours to use:	Greens/Pale blue

	Metal
Supported by:	Earth
Colours to use:	Yellow/Brown
Controlling:	Wood
Colours to use:	Green/Pale colours
Exhausted by:	Water
Colours to use:	Black/Navy Blue
Destroyed by:	Fire
Colours to use:	Red/Pink/Purple

The Eight Aspirations Formula

	Water
Supported by:	Metal
Colours to use:	White/Metallic colours
Controlling:	Fire
Colours to use:	Red/Pink/Purple
Exhausted by:	Wood
Colours to use:	Greens/Pale blue
Destroyed by:	Earth
Colours to use:	Yellow/Brown

	Wood
Supported by:	Water
Colours to use:	Black/Navy Blue
Controlling:	Earth
Colours to use:	Yellow/Brown
Exhausted by:	Fire
Colours to use:	Red/Pink/Purple
Destroyed by:	Metal
Colours to use:	White/Metallic colours

	Fire
Supported by:	Wood
Colours to use:	Greens/Pale blue
Controlling:	Metal
Colours to use:	White/Metallic colours
Exhausted by:	Earth
Colours to use:	Yellow/Brown
Destroyed by:	Water
Colours to use:	Black/Navy Blue

People are incredibly sensitive to colour; it is probably one of the quickest and easiest way to implement Feng Shui as a cure or enhancer. A dash of vibrant colour will send a powerful message to the brain. Colour communicates with the body as a sequence of vibrations, every different colour vibrates at its own unique frequency and the eyes, brain and body respond to those vibrations and interpret them as a colour, with all of its associations. By using colours with their elemental associations, you will stimulate the brain and related thought patterns. Once activated, colours, the subtle aspiration energies and their related compass directions will provide powerful Chi which works with the vital energy of the body and the building, generating opportunities for each aspiration that has been activated.

A general guide to colour and the brain's interpretations of it are:

Red

This colour vibrates at the lowest frequency, which enables the brain to read the signal at a faster rate. This means that red has an extremely high impact on the body, and it is a bold statement. It is the most yang of all colours and will provide the most stimulation and strongest energy boost.

Red is associated with vitality, sexual drive, warmth, bravery and determination. It is also the colour that represents spontaneity and happiness. However, if this colour is used in excess, the energy will spill over into a negative form and will encourage angry outbursts, headaches, tension and frustration.

This colour should be used to increase warmer tones in a cold or dark room. It is a popular colour to use as an enhancer for money (used in the southeast), travel (used in the east), recognition and fame (used in the south) because of the stimulating effect that it has on the wood and fire elements.

Pink

This colour carries a similar energy to that of red, however the effect is more gentle, as pink is the colour associated with nurturing and love. Pink has long associations with femininity and romance. It would be most effective as a choice of colour for a bedroom or playroom.

This colour is effective when used as a cure or enhancer to raise the energy associated with love, relationships and marriage when used in the southwest, as the gentle fire quality of this colour will give constant support to the earth element associated with this direction.

The Eight Aspirations Formula

Orange

This is a vibrant colour and the transition from fire to earth, therefore red to yellow. Orange represents a warmth, vitality and strength similar to that of red but without the basic intensity. Orange is a more grounding colour and the effect will be determined by the shade, the more vibrant the shade, the bigger the impact, the more yellow used to dilute the effect, the more grounding and nourishing the energy will be.

This colour will be effective if used in the south as a cure to gently reduce the pressure of a strenuous fire direction. Use it as an enhancer in the northeast to warm the mind whilst studying. Bright orange will be stimulating so it is useful when embarking on a new project, while a shade nearer to gold will provide longer stable support, which would be useful for learning or during exams.

Yellow

Yellow is the colour associated with joy and contentment, thought and intellect. It is creative and optimistic. Yellow is a bright, warm and welcoming colour with many uses. Symbolised by the sun, yellow will bring light and warmth into an area so this energy is useful in a dark or cold room.

Perhaps the best location for yellow is at the main entrance of your home, as yellow will magnify space and encourage people to relax and feel at ease. Yellow used in a lounge or conference room will stimulate the mind and body into communication and discussion; this is perfect for social and business occasions.

Using yellow as an enhancer will be useful in areas such as the southwest and northeast (earth elements), and the west and northwest (metal elements) to raise energy levels. As a cure, yellow should be used in the south to reduce the intensity of the fire energy and thus relieve pressures from work or in the north to break up the dark and receptive yin quality of the water element, like the sun shining through storm clouds. This is effective if your energy is being drained by demands from your career, or if you are feeling low or depressed.

Green

This is a colour that is associated with healing, harmony, care and growth. Green will encourage balance and stimulate the mind into openness and renewed vigour. It is a relaxing and receptive colour. It would suit the bedroom, bathroom, child's playroom and dining room.

This colour will be effective when used to give strength and support in the southeast for wealth and prosperity or in the east for health and family-related matters. Green can also be used effectively in the south if you want to obtain fame and recognition as the green wood element feeds the fire quality of the south.

If you want to use green as a cure, you should place it into the west when tension between family members exists and in the northwest if you want to reduce a constantly ringing telephone. Green placed in the north will give a fresh and creative boost to your career as it will act as an outlet for the water energy.

Blue

This is the colour that will trigger thought patterns associated with peace, calm and tranquillity. It also the colour that will slow the pace when things are too active and hectic. It is pacifying.

Blue is a colour that stimulates healing and protection. It would be a positive colour to use in the bedroom, as it will promote sleep. Blue is represented by the water element, and so can be used as an enhancer for the wood element. To have objects that are blue in the southeast or east will increase the aspirations associated with those directions.

To use blue as a cure would mean to have a blue object in the west and northwest, this will absorb any tension that may have developed in the family or office, by stimulating people to talk about their problems.

The Eight Aspirations Formula

Grey and Metallic Colours

Grey as a colour has a neutral effect, there are no stimulating qualities to grey whatsoever. However it can be used to tone down a room that is perhaps extremely fiery. Grey should be used in small doses, such as in accessories, rather than a block colour for a wall, otherwise the effect will be quite depressing and will actually drain energy away from a person or building.

Metallic colours will have more of a dramatic effect, especially gold or bronze, which will encourage the mind to think in lavish and luxurious thought patterns. Silver, chrome or galvanised zinc will bring a very modern and contemporary feel to the room, with its hard and reflective surface. As Feng Shui enhancers, metallic colours or objects will bring strength and support to the west and the northwest. These are the directions which relate to the family and communication with others. As cures for a negative energy, these colours can be used in the south as an outlet, the southeast and east to control spending and in the southwest to relieve jealousy. If metallic objects are placed in the northeast they will activate the energy associated with inner peace, therefore a metal religious statue or symbol place in this area will be very powerful.

Black

This is another colour that does little to stimulating the brain but rather acts in reverse, bringing the energy associated with stillness and quiet. It would be a suitable colour to use for toning down an active room. For example, should you have a bright sunny lounge located in the southern area of your home and your choice of colours was reds, oranges or yellows, you would need to think seriously about having a large black rug or black furniture to regain a degree of balance. This is a popular colour scheme used frequently in interiors to encourage an oriental-style atmosphere. The powerful and dramatic contrast in colours creates an air of the exotic and mystery. However, it could be too strong for a home and would better suit a restaurant or theatre.

The Eight Aspirations Formula

Black accessories can be used to give support to the north to give weight to the career. If used in the southeast or east, it will enhance the wealth and health energies as water supports wood in the Constructive Cycle of elements. Use black as a cure in the west and northwest as an outlet for pressure relating to human harmony and it can be used in the northeast to aid meditation.

White

White is reflective and spacious, it will enlarge an area that is small or awkward. It is linked to purity, virginity and cleanliness. However, white will show up any grubbiness by highlighting and magnify any flaws that may exist in the room. White can often be a cold and hard colour and so should only be used as a backdrop to other more vibrant colours. To use white effectively as an enhancer would be to increase the metal directions of west and northwest, as white is associated with this element. White can be used to support the career sector in the north as it will offer light energy into this otherwise dark element, and will follow the Constructive Cycle with metal supporting the water element.

As a cure, white can be used to create an air of quiet but dedicated calm and efficient organisation, and is therefore seen frequently in offices and hospitals.

To use colour in conjunction with items that are naturally made of the five elements in their correct positions will maximise this powerful Feng Shui formula. Once used accurately, with a balance between yin and yang, the Eight Aspirations or Compass School will quickly bring your aspirations towards you.

The Eight Aspirations Formula can be used on the whole surface area of your property or on a smaller scale, such as one room. With accurate measurements and compass directions, you will be able to increase the energy associated with each aspiration on the Bagua. Every time you pass a cure or activator, especially one that uses movement, sound or colour, you will have a constant representation of this formula and the Chi will grow and grow, eventually manifesting into physical form.

Symbolic Feng Shui

The Symbolic School has proved to be another popular form of Feng Shui. The theory behind this school is similar to that of the Eight Aspirations Formula, but instead of using just the five elements and colours, it relies on symbolic statues, articles and signs placed in the appropriate areas. Some are more popular than others, and many have superstitious or religious connections.

Below are some of the more favoured items:

Wealth

- Three Chinese coins tied together with red string or ribbon. These symbolise money being attracted to you. They can be placed in your purse, cash register or in the southeast to stimulate this sector.
- The Three-Legged Toad God. This is a small statue of a figure sitting on a pile of gold with a coin jutting out of its mouth. This statue should be placed opposite the main entrance, to the left, and will encourage money

into the building.

- Coins and bells on red string. Tied to the main entrance of your home or business these will represent incoming money and good news, especially every time the bells are activated.

Symbolic Feng Shui

- The 'Fook' sign. This is the Chinese calligraphy for prosperity, and the most auspicious sign would be painted on red paper in either black ink or gold paint.
- 'Gold' ingots. Placed in the home or office these will stimulate wealth and prosperity.
- An image of a waterfall or stream, with the flow of water towards you. This is symbolic of wealth coming to you rather than flowing away.
- Plants and flowers. These will symbolise growing and active energy. They will affect your bank balance when placed in the southeast of your home or business. They can also be placed in the hall or reception area to promote a feel-good factor and a warm welcome. It is possible to personalise flower displays to increase the energy. For example, a popular money plant is known as the Jade plant which can be found in most garden centres.
- Aquariums. Ideally these should containing filtered water and nine fish; the most auspicious combination being eight red fish and one black one. If an aquarium is unsuitable, a painting of the same will be beneficial.

A statue or image of the Chinese God Fuk. This will encourage wealth and prosperity when placed in the main living room or near the main entrance. Place Fuk with the two other gods – Luk, the god of high ranking and good fortune, and Sau the god of health and longevity.

Relationships

Rose Quartz. This pink semi-precious stone should be

placed in the southwest sector of your home or room. The southwest is an earth sector and the use of rose quartz will provide support for this element.

- A Pair of Mandarin Ducks. These represent eternal love and affection. For the pair to be effective there must be a representation of the male and the female. They should be placed in the southwest of your home or bedroom.

- The 'Double Happiness' calligraphy. This can be hung in the southwest sector of the lounge or bedroom. The sign is normally on red paper using black ink or gold paint.

- Peony flowers or images of them. These have powerful symbolic value as romantic Feng Shui enhancers, placed in the southwest of the lounge or bedroom.

Stability and Support

- The Tortoise. This is an extremely popular statue as it represents the celestial Tortoise as found in the Form or Landscape School. This should be placed behind you when you are sitting at your desk or in the north sector of your home.

- An image of a mountain. When placed behind you at your desk, this will be symbolic of stability and support.
- A statue or image of the Chinese god Luk. Luk is the god of high ranking and good fortune and a statue should be placed in the main living room or near the main entrance. This statue should be placed with the two other gods Sau and Fuk.

Health

- Jade. This stone represents health and longevity. A set of nine jade Chinese coins tied together with red string will be very auspicious, especially when placed in the east sector of the home.
- An image or statue of a crane. The crane is associated with longevity.
- Plants and flowers. These symbolise fresh growing

Symbolic Feng Shui

and active energy, providing that the plants or flowers have not passed their best. The bigger and brighter the display, the more energy is generated.

- A statue or image of the Chinese God Sau. Again, this should be placed in the main living room or near the main entrance with the two other gods Luk and Fuk.

Travel

- An image or statue of running horses. This is a very popular symbol and will also stimulate change and movement. This will be very auspicious when placed in the south sector of your home.

- A Globe. This should be placed in the east sector of your home or office. If possible, get a globe that will swivel on its axis or one that has a light inside. This enhancer will then be more effective every time you turn the light on or turn the globe. If turning the globe you must do so at least three times to generate effective Chi.

- Images of aeroplanes and exotic destinations. These

can be placed in the east sector of your home or office to symbolise travel.

Children

* A statue of laughing Buddha surrounded by children. This should be placed in a family room such as a the living room or in a child's bedroom or playroom.

A Step-by-Step Guide to Applying the Feng Shui Formulas

1. Physical Requirements

a. Exterior Environment

Examine the landscape around the building. Ideally the property should be in an 'Armchair Configuration', with support at the back (the Turtle), an open space at the front containing a small mound (the Phoenix) and 'armrests' to the sides (the Dragon and the Tiger).

A building, hill or other structure at the back of the house, will represent the Turtle and provide support to the household. If the property is missing this support it must be recreated. Feng Shui cures include a fence, wall or hedge, placing a statue of a turtle for symbolic value and adding lighting to slow Chi and increase yang energy.

Are there structures representing the Dragon and Tiger? Is the Dragon larger than the Tiger? If the Dragon and Tiger are missing they will need to be recreated by altering the landscape, constructing a fence, wall or hedge in the grounds of the property. Otherwise cures can be used in the interior of the house.

The shape and direction of roads and rivers must also be taken into consideration. The most auspicious Feng Shui will have the road or river in front of the property. If there is a road or river behind the property, steps must be taken to obscure the view, to reduce unstable energy undermining the support of the household.

b. Remedies for Exterior Poison Arrows

Poison arrows generate negative Chi; the distance and size of the poison arrows will have bearing on the effect of the Sha Chi entering the building. If there are poison arrows visible from the front entrance or windows there are steps to take to suppress their negative influence. These are:

- Block out the poison arrow with a hedge, fence or wall.
- Reflect energy back to source using a Bagua mirror.

Applying the Feng Shui Formulas

- Place protective Kirin or Temple Dogs at the entrance.
- Keep the main entrance closed and use another entrance.
- Use obscure glass and/or material to block the view of the poison arrow.

The path leading to the main entrance is important, ideally the path should be curved, facing an auspicious direction. There should be healthy plants around the front of the building to encourage positive energy.

Once the landscape surrounding the property has been identified and the Chi valued, it is then possible to move into the interior of the building.

c. Interiors – Locations, Poison Arrows and Flow of Energy

The first consideration will be the doorway and entrance, the most auspicious being a wide opening, which is bright and spacious. There should be a balance between the yin and yang energies of this area. If the area is too dark, a light should be left on to encourage yang energy.

Energy should be able to flow freely into and around the building, so note obstructions and possible antidotes. This rule applies to all of the rooms in the property.

If the staircase is opposite the front door, you must place a cure to reduce Chi from rushing straight to the upper floors. A plant or wind chime near this point will slow down the Chi.

Moving slowly from room to room, note the positions of the furniture and whether there are poison arrows caused by sharp angles from walls, beams or furniture. If there are, are the poison arrows directed at the seating or sleeping positions of the household? If so, what steps can be taken to remove the negative effect? Can the furniture be moved away from the poison arrow? Is it possible to cover sharp angles with material? Can plants or statues be placed in between the poison arrows and people?

2. The Feng Shui Formulas

a. Eight Mansions – Placing People

Once you are satisfied with the physical energy flowing in and around your property and have implemented remedies where necessary, you begin to activate some of the secret formulas that will enable you to tap into the energy of the earth.

Everybody will have a Kua number that will give four favourable directions to face and four unfavourable directions which should be avoided. These directions can be applied to the entrance of the building, and are recommended for seating and sleeping positions. To tap into auspicious luck you should sit facing one of your best directions. If this is not currently possible, change the positioning of the furniture to allow the best arrangement. There must still be room for a free flow of energy and you must avoid creating poison arrows.

Reduce overcrowding and keep a balance between yin and yang for all rooms. Concentrate on the main earner in the home or power figure in the business first, then apply the rules to the other members of the family or employees in their own rooms.

b. Life Aspirations – Placing Objects

The next formula will rely on intentions and the related directions of the Bagua. This formula should only be activated in the yang rooms, such as the hall, lounge, study, playroom and dining room. There are eight sectors, which can be activated; all are sensitive to the five elements. By placing symbolic objects and remedies relating to the Constructive or Destructive Cycles of elements in their allocated directions, you will increase the energy relating to each aspiration.

3. Check List

Use this checklist as a guide, as it will ensure that you cover all of the important points and are less likely to make mistakes.

Applying the Feng Shui Formulas

Landscape

1. Is there a structure representing the Celestial Turtle at the back of the house?

       Yes ☐   No ☐

If not, can one be introduced?

       Yes ☐   No ☐

2. Are there structures to the left and right of your building, representing the Celestial Dragon and Tiger?

Dragon: Yes ☐   No ☐

Tiger: Yes ☐   No ☐

If not, can they be introduced?

       Yes ☐   No ☐

3. Is the structure representing the Dragon larger than the Tiger?

       Yes ☐   No ☐

If not, what steps must you take to reduce the
negative effect?

....

4. Is there an open space in front of the house or
main door?

        Yes ❏   No ❏

If not, what steps can you use to make the
area appear brighter?

....

5. Is there a representation of the Celestial
Phoenix?

        Yes ❏   No ❏

Is it possible to build a small mound of red
flowers in this area?

        Yes ❏   No ❏

Applying the Feng Shui Formulas

6. Are there any water features near the property?

                Yes ☐   No ☐

If so, is the water in front of the property?

                Yes ☐   No ☐

Is the water behind the property?

                Yes ☐   No ☐

If so, what steps can be taken to reduce the effect of unstable support?

....

7. List any poison arrows in front of the house.

....

....

....

What steps can be taken to reduce their negative effect?

....

8. What is the position of the road in front of the main door?

> Direction ....
>
> Shape.....................

9. How is the house positioned in relation to the road?

Direction facing.......................................

Distance from road ....

10. Is main entrance in proportion to the rest of the building?

> Yes ☐   No ☐

Direction the door is facing ....

11. Are there any poison arrows in front of the door or windows?

> Yes ☐   No ☐

Applying the Feng Shui Formulas

What can be done to reduce their effect?

....

12. Is there a path to the entrance?

        Yes ☐   No ☐

13. Is the path straight or curved?

....

14. Are there plants and wildlife?

        Yes ☐   No ☐

15. Is there adequate lighting?

        Yes ☐   No ☐

16. Does the property have any missing corners?

        Yes ☐   No ☐

17. Are there any existing Feng Shui cures in place?

Yes ☐   No ☐

18. If cures are in place, are they effective for their original purpose?

Yes ☐   No ☐

19. Note any further relevant information.

… …..

…………………………………………………………

…………………………………………………………

…………………………………………………………

Interiors

1. Main Entrance: Is the main entrance bright, open and spacious?

Yes ☐   No ☐

Applying the Feng Shui Formulas

2. What is the position of the staircase in relation to main entrance?

> Straight or curved ....
> Distance from entrance ....

3. Is it possible to see the back door from the entrance?

> Yes ☐   No ☐

4. Are there any poison arrows directed at any of the sitting or sleeping positions?

> Yes ☐   No ☐

5. Is it possible to reduce their effect?

> Yes ☐   No ☐

6. Are there any negative areas?

> Yes ☐   No ☐

7. Is it possible to improve these areas?

Yes ☐   No ☐

8. Is there a balance between yin and yang in the décor in every room?

Yes ☐   No ☐

9. Can changes be made to bring balance between the yin and yang energies?

Yes ☐   No ☐

10. Is there a fresh flow of air?

Yes ☐   No ☐

11. If not, what can you do to release stale or stagnant energy?

…………......................…………………………….

12. Living Room: What is the position of the living room in relation to the house?

Applying the Feng Shui Formulas

Sector ....

13. Is this sector beneficial compared against the Kua Directions for the family members?

....

....

....

....

....

....

14. What are the sitting directions for the people using this room?

....

....

....

....

....

....

15. Are the seating positions correct for favourable Kua Directions?

Yes ☐   No ☐

16. Is it possible to move the sitting positions to be more favourable?

Yes ☐   No ☐

17. Can Feng Shui remedies or cures enhance the Chi or activate an aspiration in this room?

Yes ☐   No ☐

18. Dining Room: What is the position of this room in relation to the house?

Sector ....

19. Is this sector beneficial compared against the Kua Directions for the family members?

....

....

Applying the Feng Shui Formulas

....
....
....
....

20. What are the sitting directions for the people using this room?

....
....
....
....
....
....

21. Are the positions correct for favourable Kua Directions?

Yes ☐   No ☐

22. Is it possible to move the positions to be more favourable?

        Yes ☐   No ☐

23. Can Feng Shui remedies or cures enhance the Chi or activate an aspiration in this room?

        Yes ☐   No ☐

24. Bedrooms: What are the positions of these rooms in relation to the house?

Sector ....

Sector ....

Sector ....

Sector ....

Sector ....

Sector ....

25. Are these sectors beneficial compared against the Kua Directions for the family members?

Applying the Feng Shui Formulas

....
....
....
....
....

26. What are the sleeping directions for the
people using these room?

....
....
....
....
....
....

27. Are the positions correct for favourable Kua
Directions?

        Yes ☐   No ☐

28. Is it possible to move the positions to be more favourable?

Yes ☐   No ☐

29. Can Feng Shui remedies or cures enhance the Chi in these room?

Yes ☐   No ☐

30. Kitchen: What is the position of this room in relation to the house?

Sector ....

31. Is this sector beneficial compared against the Kua Directions for the family members?

....
....
....
....
....
....

Applying the Feng Shui Formulas

32. What direction is the energy entering the oven and electrical appliances?

....

....

....

....

33. Bathroom: What is the position of this room in relation to the house?

Sector ....

34. Is this sector beneficial compared against the Kua Directions for the family members?

....

....

....

....

....

....

35. Toilet: What is the position of this room in relation to the house?

Sector ....

36. Is this sector beneficial compared against the Kua Directions for the family members?

....

....

....

....

....

37. Garage: What is the position of this room in relation to the house?

Sector ....

38. Is this sector beneficial compared against the Kua Directions for the family members?

....

....

Applying the Feng Shui Formulas

....
....
....
....

39. Storeroom: What is the position of this room
in relation to the house?

       Sector ....

40. Is this sector beneficial compared against the
Kua Directions for the family members?

....
....
....
....
....

41. Greenhouse: What is the position of this
room in relation to the house?

       Sector ....

42. Is this sector beneficial compared against the
Kua Directions for the family members?

....

....

....

....

....

Troubleshooting

It is impossible to have a home or office that is totally full of auspicious Chi, as there must always be a small part of yin inside every yang. There are some rules of Feng Shui that are more important than others, and so if there are problems in your Feng Shui, you must prioritise them and look at ways to reduce the negative effect.

Before you can work on the interior of the building you must measure the level of energy that is outside, for it is this energy that will waft in and around your home and business. Every time you enter or leave the building you will be encountering this Chi and its effects. Here are a few tips you can use to reduce the possibility of trouble before it enters the home.

- The outside of your home should be as attractive as possible, with an abundance of plants and wildlife. Go for evergreens that will provide a constant green foliage. These are perfect for representing the Dragon to the left of your property.

- Have a curved path leading to your door, this will naturally slow Chi into valuable energy, before it enters the building.

- Fix any broken items or odd jobs that remain outside, these could include broken steps or cracked paving, weeds across the path, a faulty doorbell or a broken light. All of these will generate an air of neglect and a lack of concern, not the message you want to convey.

- Keep the entrance as bright as possible. This means leaving a light on in the porch at all times, even during the day. Remember that a light will generate positive yang energy which will accumulate at your door. Every time you open your door to leave or enter you will allow this energy access to the building.

- Remove any foliage or structure that is obstructing entry to your building, this could be in the form of a hanging branch or overgrown shrubs, it could also be a dustbin left carelessly on the path.

If you are suffering from an external poison arrow opposite your main entrance, you must take the necessary steps to reduce the effect of cutting Shar Chi.

Troubleshooting

Again this is to protect the interior of the building by addressing the problem from outside. In extreme cases, where no natural remedies, such as a hedge, are possible, you may hang a reflective Bagua mirror to reflect the unfavourable Chi back to its source.

The next stage is the interior of your home or business. Consider the first impressions, and imagine that you are a stranger visiting the property for the first time.

- What impression of the inhabitants does the building give you?
- What was the first item that you noticed on entering?
- Does the house or office look bright and welcoming?
- What was the first aroma that you picked up, was it dampness, floral, incense, musty, doggy?
- What colours have been used? Are they in harmony? How do they make you feel?
- What impressions do you get from the building? Do your feel relaxed and peaceful or frustrated and anxious?
- What sounds are noticeable, a hum of electrical

items, children playing, music, trickling water?

- Are there any flowers or plants in this area? If so, are they happy and healthy or past their best and gloomy and depressed?
- What behaviour do you notice about the inhabitants of this building (this could include children and pets if applicable)? Are they settled and happy, hyperactive or lazy and lethargic?

Once you feel comfortable that you have identified the quality of the Chi in and around your building and the knock-on effect that it has on your home, you can look at ways for improvement where necessary. Identifying areas of trouble and shooting them down is an important aspect of Feng Shui before you implement any of the formulas or enhancers.

Dos and Don'ts

On the whole, Feng Shui is extremely adaptable and flexible, its uniqueness stems from the ability to tailor positive Feng Shui adjustments to any individual person or property. Whatever the problem, Feng Shui, once implemented correctly, will make massive improvements immediately after application. However, there are some cures or enhancers that should be treated with a little more respect and consideration than others, these include:

Bagua Mirrors

The Bagua Mirror is a powerful spiritual tool. There are several available styles, all of which have a mirror in the centre surrounded by a sequence of trigrams. It is the correct sequence of the trigrams that holds the key to spiritual values, and will act as a protector against evil forces or spirits.

The early heaven sequence

Some Bagua mirrors are flat; these will reflect exactly the image that is opposite them, without any distortion. Other Bagua mirrors include a convex mirror, where the glass is curving outwards, and they will draw a larger image to the trigrams and send an extended reflection back across a wider field.

The other type of mirror is a concave Bagua mirror; this has the glass curved inward. It will draw the image into the centre of the trigrams and hold it there, trapped. This type of mirror will be best used when there is a negative image opposite your entrance.

Dos and Don'ts

You must make sure that the Trigrams are positioned correctly in the format that is known as the Early Heaven Sequence, otherwise the Bagua mirror will not work. Another important rule is that the Bagua mirror with the correct trigrams should only be used outside the building and should never be hung inside.

Mirrors

Ordinary mirrors are powerful Feng Shui cures and enhancers. They work as reflectors and will double any image opposite them. To use mirrors correctly it is important that the image that you want reflected is positive, such as a dining table or a cash register. But use them wisely, if they are positioned opposite the front door they will immediately reflect the incoming Chi of your building straight back outside. If they are hung in the bedroom opposite the bed, they will reflect the energy that you are releasing through dreams back into your body. This will cause confusion to you whilst you sleep, as your subconscious is discarding all of the unneeded information that you picked up during the course of the day and the mirror is reflecting it straight back into your energy field. How confusing! You will wake up feeling heavy and dazed instead of waking refreshed.

Take Your Time

When you first begin to alter the Feng Shui of your environment, you must take your time. Do not be tempted to rush into spending thousands of pounds or have sleepless nights worrying that everything inside and outside your home needs a radical change. It is when a person acts in haste that mistakes are made.

Preparation and growing awareness of your home and the energy that it attracts will take time. Begin gradually, starting with the basics. Space clearing will be a wonderful way of preparing to energise your home using Feng Shui. Removing clutter is similar to exfoliating dead skin cells, be honest and set yourself a target, if it hasn't been used in a year or more, then you don't need it. This will open your mind, cupboards and wardrobes to receiving the new and fresh opportunities that positive Feng Shui will stimulate.

Proportion

This is imperative, should you plant an evergreen outside your home to generate and accumulate positive Chi, you must make sure that in ten years' time this opportunity enhancer hasn't grown to become a dark and menacing figure dominating the front of your house. An overgrown tree will prevent Chi and especially sunlight (yang Chi) access through the doors and windows. This rule applies to hedges, walls, neighbouring structures, buildings, electricity pylons, anything that is in your immediate vicinity. Use proportion inside the home or office as well, dark and heavy furniture will be oppressive, especially when crammed into a room, therefore only use this type of furniture in spacious rooms.

Invisible Feng Shui – It's All About Balance

It is possible for you to fill your home and business with symbolic Chinese artefacts, using your best intentions, and placing them carefully in their specified Feng Shui directions and over time they will work and increase the subtle energy fields. The only problem is that this approach is only surface Feng Shui.

For far-reaching and long-term results, you need a deeper understanding and awareness of the environment that you are spending time in. You are continually absorbing information and collecting energy from your environment. By increasing the natural rhythms and patterns of nature by supporting them with natural products carrying similar energy vibrations, you will be working Feng Shui at a deeper level.

The rules for yin and yang, the five elements and avoiding poison arrows will bring balance and harmony to your home before you activate the Eight Mansions,

Eight Aspirations and Symbolic Schools. Invisible Feng Shui is natural, as is the Chi emanating from the heavens and the earth, the rivers and mountains. To tap into and harness favourable Chi you must consider your natural resources and then the location and position of your property, and find a balance. Over time, as your awareness grows, you will be able to make slight adjustments to further the benefit of harmonised Chi.

Natural Remedies – What to Expect

Raising Your Awareness

When you first begin to implement Feng Shui you are already becoming increasingly aware of how your surrounding and environment can exert powerful influential forces on you. Your awareness has already grown for you to consider using Feng Shui as a tool. Over a period of time, you will start to become even more sensitive as subtle changes begin to open up around you. As you finely tune your environment, you may notice that a particular aspect of your life has blossomed and grown since you activated an area in your space.

How Sensitive is the Feng Shui of Your Home, Office, Business, Garden, Body and Car?

These are questions you can ask yourself if you feel that there is a problem. You may feel your potential is not being realised, or be unhappy about high running costs or sluggish production.

If there is a problem with your health or even your car, try to identify the element that it relates to, ask yourself if this element has become overpowering or neglected. By using the Constructive or Destructive Cycles of the elements, look at ways or rebalancing the negative element. This practice should not be used instead of or in place of a registered doctor or mechanic.

How the Five Elements Relate to Your Body

- Fire is the element that governs the brain, heart, nervous system and blood. If you are suffering from headaches, tension, irritability or any nervous disorder, it may be that the fire energy in your body is craving attention. You may need to increase the fire energy with more fire or support from the wood element. Experiment with wearing different colours, and check to see what colours are in your environment to find the cause of the problem.

- Earth governs the stomach, flesh, cells and digestive organs. If you are a person who easily gains weight or one who suffers from bloating or stomach cramps, you may need to rebalance the earth energy inside your body. This element is also responsible for laziness, and so if it is extreme and you are finding it difficult to get moving, you may need to give the earth element an outlet. By increasing the metal element, for instance by wearing metal jewellery, you will use up some of the excessive earth energy. Wood will absorb excess energy and so including green leafy foods in your diet will aid a weight-loss program.

- Metal governs the skin, lungs, intestines and teeth. For skin problems, indigestion or a tightening of the chest, you may need to pay attention to the metal element. As metal is supported by the earth element, it makes sense to look closely at your diet, and check the health of your stomach and digestive organs. Avoid eating hot and spicy foods as they will increase the fire element that has the power to weaken the metal element. By increasing you water intake you will give negative metal energy an outlet, and will flush out the problem.

- Water governs the kidneys, reproductive organs and the ears. If this energy has become unbalanced it will eventually cause problems in these regions. To give the water element support, you must increase the metal element. One way would be to check whether you are suffering from a mineral deficiency. An outlet for water is the wood element so eating fresh fruit and vegetables will aid recovery.

Invisible Feng Shui

- Wood governs the eyes, limbs, liver, arms, legs and neck. If you are suffering from problems of the body governed by the wood element, you may need to increase the fire energy to burn away toxins and raise your energy levels or provide support by increasing the intake of fluids to flush out any lurking germs.

How the Five Elements Relate to the Car

The Feng Shui sensitive car will mostly be governed by the metal element due the material from which it is built and the fact that it is used for connecting people to places. However, even in a car you can find the other elements:

- Fire will be activated if the car is red; this will encourage the driver to drive faster. Fire will also relate to the engine and spark plugs, they do not respond well to the influence of a damp, cold water energy such as that found on a winter's morning as demonstrated by the Destructive Cycle of elements.
- Earth will be activated if the colour of the car is yellow

through to shades of brown. Drivers of these colour cars will tend to be safe and reliable. The seats are governed by this element, and so a car with high levels of this energy will be comfortable. If this car were square in shape it would reinforce the earth element and this would encourage slow and methodical driving.

- Metal will be even more powerful if the colour of the car is white or metallic. The structure and all electrical switches and wiring of the car are governed by this element. A highly technical car will have high levels of metal energy and so would require a calm and efficient personality to master all of the controls.

- Water is an outlet for the metal element, and so black or navy will be Feng Shui friendly colours for a car, as they will encourage the driver to relax and drive carefully. The radiator, heater and all fluids in the car are governed by this element. Water is supported by the metal element and the metal element will govern the connectors, tubing and pipes. If water is unable to circulate there may be an air block in one of the connectors. To keep your car in perfect condition, make sure that all of the fluids are kept topped up and provide regular oil changes.

- Wood is the element represented by shades of green. Wood will stimulate action from the metal element, therefore driving a green car will be stimulating to the driver. The carburettor, filter and wheels are governed by this element. The wood element is associated with health, and so to keep your car healthy it is advisable to use lead-free petrol. Wood cars tend to be fuel-effective, with more miles to the gallon. If your car is guzzling gas you may need to look for leaks, cracks and strains, which are signs of a weak wood element. Clean fluids will give strong water energy support as demonstrated in the Constructive Cycle of elements.

Experimentation and Having Fun

Feng Shui should be fun, it is a serious subject and for you to use Feng Shui successfully takes a certain degree of responsibility, but that does not mean that it should eliminate fun.

The most effective way to lift your spirits is through laughter. Doctors and scientists have proven that laughter is the body's natural way to reduce tension and stress that would otherwise encourage the on-set of illness. If your are feeling unhappy toward a particular aspect of your life, the quickest way to address the problem is to introduce an item into the home that will make you smile.

If you are worried about the existing Feng Shui of your home, or worried that the cures you have placed there may not be working, you will be creating barriers for the energy to enter your own field of energy. Your thought patterns generate Chi, similar to that of an electrical signal, that connects with those of the heavens and the earth. Should your mind be filled with self-doubt and negative reactions it is unlikely that you will notice the positive energy around you. Instead you will be concentrating on finding a problem.

The best solution is to keep things simple and to experiment. Do not be tempted into construction changes to your home unless that is what you really want deep down.

Gradually you will begin to notice a change to the way you feel. Others will mention that you are looking brighter. People will treat you with respect and admiration and, in turn, you will become more confident and self-assured. You will then begin to recognise that this is just the beginning of the Feng Shui working for you.

Remind Yourself That You Are Worth It

This may sound easier in theory than in practice, as we are constantly pushed into a competitive cycle by the demands and expectations of a modern society. The pressure is on to have the best, be the best and be constantly better than your competitors, without any obvious pit stop to convalesce or recharge your energy levels. This is why Feng Shui has grown at such an accelerated rate recently, as it enables you to tap into the available natural resources in your own home. Feng Shui will provide you with an endless stream of positive energy.

The History of the Classical Feng Shui

Legends and Mystic Masters

There is a legend that the secrets of Feng Shui were encoded in a mysterious shroud that was found hidden in a cave, deep in a mountain. It is said that there were several branches of secrets all relating to the meaning of life and the steps to take for enlightenment, according to the Tao. These secrets were said to have been buried by the holy Buddha.

The legend continues that the man who found these texts took them to his homeland of China, where he unravelled the secrets and applied them to his life, his home and to his family. His life dramatically changed and news of his transformation spread rapidly until it reached the ears of the mystical Yellow Emperor. When the Yellow Emperor heard of this magical feat, he ordered guards to find the man and to bring him to his court. Afraid for his safety, he wanted the secrets for himself.

The History of the Classical Feng Shui

According to the Yellow Emperor's wishes, the man was brought to the court and instead of being persecuted he was protected and made a man of high rank, who was constantly at the Yellow Emperor's side to give advice and to perform acts of divination and predictions. It is this that is said to have made the Yellow Emperor so mystical and powerful.

There are many stories and legends that are passed down through the generations to whet the appetite and to continue the practice of Feng Shui. However, many are unfounded, often exaggerated to keep the attention of the listener. Yet Feng Shui is not a mere fabric of imagination. There are written reports and mountains of text dating back thousands of years which not only disclose the secret formulas, but often give detailed accounts of the before, during and after effects, stretching back over many dynasties. The first documents relating to the trigrams were written in 4477 BC by Fu Hsi in China and from then on many influences moulded and evolved Feng Shui into its current form.

The most powerful rulers and most affluent periods

of China's history belong to those who applied the wisdom of Feng Shui. These were periods where Feng Shui was not treated as mere superstition but was held to have the highest relevance. To protect the courts, the secrets were encoded in beautiful poetry. It is the interpretation of this poetry which has lead to present-day Feng Shui.

Perhaps the most recognised and powerful Feng Shui practitioner was Master Yang Yun-Sang who was the advisor to Emperor Hi Tsang during the wealthy Tang Dynasty (888 AD).

Original Lo-Shu and The I Ching

Another legend describes the origins of the Lo Shu magic square. It says that a sage was resting by the River Lo, in around 2005 BC, when to his surprise a giant turtle emerged from the river, carrying unusual markings on his shell. There were nine strange markings, representing the numbers one to nine, in a special pattern.

The pattern of these numbers corresponded with the

The History of the Classical Feng Shui

eight trigrams and their allocated compass directions of the Later Heaven Sequence. If the numbers of any of the lines of the square, vertical, horizontal or diagonal, were added together, the result would always be fifteen. This sequence of numbers was recognised by mystical peers and sages as holding magical properties.

Whatever its origins, the Lo Shu square became connected with the existing formulas of Feng Shui and has exerted a powerful influence in Chinese culture and Feng Shui.

A big advance in the development of Feng Shui came in The Chou Dynasty (1122 BC) when King Wen interpreted the sixty-four hexagrams that make up the I Ching. In fact, because of his impressive following, he was hailed as a rebellion leader and was captured and imprisoned for seven years. It was during this time that he actually wrote the I Ching.

The I Ching is known as the 'Book of Changes' or the ' Book of Wisdom'. After the death of King Wen, his son, the Duke of Chou, continued this impressive work. The Duke of Chou wrote the texts of the meanings behind each hexagram. It was his contribution that dramatically turned the I Ching into an oracle. After a lifetime study of the I Ching, Confucius (550 BC–479BC) attached an appendix, which is known as the Ten Wings. This has given a further insight into the sometimes obscure readings. Even today, the I Ching is used as an oracle and is being constantly consulted for valuable insight into man and his position in the universe.

Glossary of Terms

Bagua: An eight-sided symbol consisting of compass directions, the eight trigrams and corresponding elements. Used for the Eight Aspirations formula, it is derived from the I Ching.

Chi: Energy that originates from the heavens and the earth. Chi can be positive or negative.

Chueh Ming: The worst direction in the Eight Mansions formula. This direction will encourage total loss to health, prosperity and relationships. Spending time in this location will encourage disaster.

Compass School: A school of Feng Shui that concentrates on the direction of energy to encourage fortunate energy into the building. There are several branches of the Compass School, including the Eight Mansions formula and Eight Aspirations formula.

Confucius: A Chinese philosopher who lived 551–479 BC. He developed the I Ching and is a central figure to Chinese culture and the principles of Feng Shui.

Duke of Chou: the son of King Wen who wrote the texts

to each of the sixty-four hexagrams in the I Ching.

Early Heaven Arrangement: The first arrangement of trigrams which act as a description of all natural forces of energy. This sequence of numbers is used for protection against evil spirits and poison arrows. It is this arrangement that is used when calculating auspicious burial sites.

Eight Aspirations Formula: A formula of Feng Shui that uses the compass directions and the Bagua to encourage life intentions and turn them into tangible results. This formula concentrates on the five elements as tools and enhancers. It is this formula that is used for the placement of objects for Feng Shui purposes. It will take into consideration the direction of the main entrance to determine what subtle energy type is entering the building.

Eight Mansions Formula: A formula of Feng Shui that uses compass directions and time span to determine the placement of people for Feng Shui purposes. There will be four fortunate directions for every person to spend time facing and four unfortunate directions for people to avoid facing. This formula also takes into consideration the direction of the main entrance of the building to determine whether it is an auspicious for the head of the household or an unlucky direction. The five elements can be used in conjunction with this formula to increase or decrease the energy from each direction.

Elemental Energy: The five subtle types of energy: earth, metal, water, wood and fire. It is a Chinese belief that the five forces of nature combine to make the universe. Everything consists of a combination of these five elements. The elements are continually changing; they work in time cycles known as the Constructive and Destructive Cycles. Each element is as powerful and weak as another.

Feng Shui: Translated this means wind – water. It is the name given to the practice of harnessing the earth's energy. To live with positive Feng Shui is to live in harmony with nature.

Form School: A school of Feng Shui that concentrates on the natural shape and contours of the land to determine the level of fortunate and unfortunate energy that revolves in and around the building under consultation.

Fu Hsi: The legendary Chinese ruler who invented the trigrams.

Fu Wei: One of the auspicious directions used in Eight Mansions formula of Compass School. This location is for achieving inner peace and is a positive direction for learning, education and meditation.

Fuk: The Chinese god used to encourage wealth and prosperity.

Hexagram: A symbol consisting of six lines, either broken or unbroken. Altogether there are sixty-four different hexagrams, each made of two trigrams. These hexagrams form the basis of the book of the I Ching. Each hexagram is related to man, heaven, earth and consciousness.

Ho Hai: The term given to one of the inauspicious locations in the Eight Mansions formula of the Compass School. This location is related to accidents and mishaps.

Glossary of Terms

I Ching: The Book of Change, a Chinese classic written by King Wen, the Duke of Chou and Confucius. This book is central to many of the Feng Shui formulas. It is used for divination and fortune telling. It is probably the oldest book in existence.

King Wen: The man who formulated the sixty-four hexagrams that are used in the I Ching. He was the founder of the I Ching.

Kirin: The Kirin or temple dogs are a pair of auspicious mystical creatures that represent fortunate opportunities, wealth, success, longevity and family harmony. They are also used to protect the home from evil spirits and unfavourable Chi. They are normally placed either side of the main entrance looking out, or on a window sill facing external poison arrows.

Kua: One of the eight sides of the Bagua. Kua is also used in the Eight Mansions formula to determine which are a person's four fortunate directions and four unfortunate direction.

Later Heaven Arrangement: The second sequence of trigram arrangements as found in the centre of the

Bagua. It is this arrangement that is used for Feng Shui consultations for homes, gardens, offices, etc.

Lo Pan: A specialised Feng Shui compass.

Lo-Shu: The magic square. An arrangement of numbers between one and nine in a grid. The combinations of numbers are central to powerful Feng Shui formulas.

Lui Sha: One of the inauspicious directions of the Eight Mansions formula of the Compass School. This location is related to serious harm to the health, wealth and relationships of the family.

Luk: The Chinese god of power, authority and high ranking.

Master Yang Yun-Sang: A legendary Feng Shui consultant during the Tang Dynasty, when Feng Shui was highly respected and admired.

Nien Yen: One of the auspicious directions of the Eight Mansions formula of the Compass School. This location is related to the direction that promotes harmonious relationships with friends, family, partners and colleagues.

Poison Arrows: Objects that generate negative cutting

Glossary of Terms

energy. Poison arrows are straight or sharp; the Chi they create will bring ill fortune.

Ren Chai: Man luck, one of the three trinities of luck that control every person's destiny. Man luck is the luck that each person makes for him- or herself.

Sau: The Chinese god that will encourage good health and long life.

Shar Chi: Unfortunate energy, as generated by poison arrows and negative areas.

Sheng Chi: Fortunate energy that will generate positive opportunities and a feeling of wellbeing.

Tai Chi: The symbol representing the meaning of life, which consists of the two duel forces of nature, yin and yang, that are forever entwined.

Tao: Meaning 'The Way', a philosophy that takes into account the energy of the heavens and earth in harmony. It is used in the I Ching and Feng Shui .

Ti Chai : Earth luck, one of the three trinities of luck that control every person's destiny. This can be altered through the Feng Shui formulas.

Tien Chai: Heaven luck, one of the three trinities of

luck that control every person's destiny. Heaven luck is a form of astrology based on the elemental energies available at the moment of birth. It cannot be altered.

Tien Yi: One of the auspicious directions of the Eight Mansions formula of the Compass School. It is favourable for promoting good health and long life.

Trigram: A symbol consisting of three lines, either broken or unbroken, which represent heaven, earth and man in the universe. There are eight trigrams.

Wu Kwai: One of the inauspicious directions of the Eight Mansions formula of the Compass School. It is related to fire, burglary and loss of employment or income.

Yang: One of the two forces of nature. It is positive energy and can be used as a description for active, bright, loud, summer, hot and masculine forces. It is one of the two duel forces of nature.

Yin: The complement of yang. Yin can be used to describe negative, passive, dark, quiet, winter, cold and feminine forces. It is the second of the two forces of nature.

Useful Addresses

Jo Russell

Feng Shui Consultant and Four Pillars Astrologer

61 Harwater Drive

Loughton

Essex

IG10 ILP

Tel: 0208 281 9107

The Plant Studio

Feng Shui Garden Services

Unit 2, Mimram Road

Hertford

SG14 1NN

Tel: 01992 581 771

Linx (UK) Ltd

Chinese Art

Maple Drive

Kendal

Cumbria

LA9 5BN

Tel: 01539 725832

Recommended Authors

Master Raymond Lo
Lillian Too
Master Kwok Man Ho
Derek Walters
Jon Sandifer